THE
HOLIDAY
SONG BOOK

For the students at
The Studio on Eleventh Street
who are learning that we are
ultimately responsible for our
own education—
Happy Singing!

THE
HOLIDAY
SONG BOOK

100 Songs! 27 Holidays!

Selections, illustrations
and additional lyrics by

Robert Quackenbush

All music arranged
for easy piano and guitar by

Harry Buch

·

Lothrop, Lee & Shepard Company

A Division of William Morrow & Company, Inc.

NEW YORK

Featuring the Bird Players & Singers

ACKNOWLEDGMENTS: Grateful appreciation is expressed by the author to the publishers who have so kindly lent the following songs for inclusion in this book: "My Dreydl," taken from *The Songs We Sing* by Harry Coopersmith: United Synagogue of America, reprinted by permission of the Board of Jewish Education of Greater New York; "Birthday Song," from *Book I—Music Through the Day* in the *Music For Living Series*, 1956, by permission of Silver Burdett Company, New York; "Navajo Happy Song," recorded by Marguerite Twohy in New Mexico: reprinted from the *Girl Scout Pocket Songbook* by permission of the National Headquarters of the Girl Scouts of the United States of America; "The Caissons Go Rolling Along," by permission of Shapiro, Bernstein & Co., Inc., New York; "Arbor Day Song," from *Book 3: Exploring Music Series*, 1966, reprinted by permission of Holt, Rinehart & Winston, Publishers, New York; "Hanukkah Song" and "Preparing for Seder," from *The Gateway to Jewish Song* by Judith Eisenstein, by permission of Behrman House, Inc., Publishers, New York.

Further appreciation is extended to Mr. Robert Welber and the students at Mr. Welber's elementary school, *The Studio on Eleventh Street* in New York City, for their helpful suggestions; Patricia Lanari, Silvia Barros (Professor, Hofstra University, New York), Beatrice Cole (Professor, Instituto de Allende, San Miguel, Mexico), and Mrs. C. de Nivón (Hispanic Museum, New York City) for their valuable help in translating Latin American songs; Rudolph Hahn for his assistance with German translations; Martha Lyons and Beatrice Cole for their assistance in selecting and translating the Hebrew songs; Kitty Kirby of WNYC radio station, New York, for her valuable suggestions for the Dr. Martin Luther King, Jr.'s Birthday section; the staff at the Museum of the American Indian's library in Bronx, New York, for their helpful recommendations for the American Indian Day section. In addition, valuable suggestions and contributions were made by the staff at the main branch of the Jacksonville Public Library, Jacksonville, Florida; the librarians who attended the conference at the 1976 Kentucky Media Association; the librarians who attended the programs at the August 1976 meetings held at the Los Angeles and Long Beach Public Libraries; and the staffs of the following New York City Public Libraries: the 42nd Street Research Division, the Children's Division of Donnell Library, the Children's Division of the Yorkville Branch, the Webster Branch, and the Lincoln Center Library of the Performing Arts.

Deepest appreciation and warmest thanks are extended to Harry Buch, who arranged and hand-drew all the music in this book, and to Philip Bouwsma, who hand-lettered the lyrics and song titles, and to Carol Barkin, who checked every detail from start to finish.

1 2 3 4 5 6 7 8 9 10

LIBRARY OF CONGRESS CATALOGING IN PUBLICATION DATA
Main entry under title: The Holiday song book. Includes index.
SUMMARY: Includes 100 songs for celebrating twenty-seven different holidays.
1. Children's songs.   2. Holidays—Songs and music.
[1. Songs.   2. Holidays—Songs and music]   I. Quackenbush, Robert M.   II. Buch, Harry.
M1997.H   784.6   77-5895   ISBN 0-688-41820-1   ISBN 0-688-51820-6 lib. bdg.

CONTENTS

NEW YEAR'S DAY	7
Wassail Song	8
The Bells on New Year's Day	9
Auld Lang Syne	10
DR. MARTIN LUTHER KING, JR.'S BIRTHDAY	11
We Can Overcome	12
He's Got This Whole World in His Hands	13
Michael, Row the Boat Ashore	14
ABRAHAM LINCOLN'S BIRTHDAY	15
Lincoln and Liberty	16
Out from the Wilderness	17
The Battle Hymn of the Republic	18
VALENTINE'S DAY	19
Mister Frog Went A-Courting	20
A Paper of Pins	21
Love Somebody, Yes I Do	22
Billy Boy	22
GEORGE WASHINGTON'S BIRTHDAY	23
Yankee Doodle	24
Chester	25
Washington the Great	26
SAINT PATRICK'S DAY	27
Saint Patrick Was a Gentleman	28
Cockles and Mussels	29
Michael Finnegan	30
APRIL FOOLS' DAY	31
There's a Hole in Our Bucket	32
There's a Flea in Lizzie's Ear	33
This Ol' Man	34
PAN-AMERICAN DAY	35
Cielito Lindo	36
Chacarera	37
La Cucaracha	38
EASTER	39
Easter Hymn	40
O Glorious Bells of Easter	41
Easter Basket	42
Itisket, Itasket	42
PASSOVER	43
Preparing for Seder	44
Go Down, Moses	45
Dayenu	46
ARBOR DAY / EARTH DAY	47
Deep in the Woods	48
Arbor Day Song	49
It's the Same the Whole World Over	50
MAY DAY	51
Three Little Girls	52
Now Is the Month of Maying	53
Today's the First of May	54
MOTHER'S DAY	55
Mary	56
Mama's Gonna Buy	57
Hush, Little Baby	57
My Mom Won't Allow	58
MEMORIAL DAY	59
Tenting on the Old Camp Ground	60
When Johnny Comes Marching Home Again	61
Taps	62
Tramp! Tramp! Tramp!	62
FLAG DAY	63
The Star-Spangled Banner	64
The Red, White, and Blue	65
You're a Grand Old Flag	66

FATHER'S DAY 67
Daddy Wouldn't Buy Me a Bow Wow 68
Watching for Pa 69
Daddy's Whiskers (1) 70
Daddy's Whiskers (2) 71
Love My Daddy, Yes I Do 71
The No, No, Yes, Yes Aria 72

INDEPENDENCE DAY 73
America the Beautiful 74
Yankee Doodle Boy 75
America 76

LABOR DAY 77
Erie Canal 78
Blow the Man Down 79
I've Been Working on the Railroad 80
Git Along, Little Dogies 81
Down the River 82

AMERICAN INDIAN DAY 83
Sioux Night Song 84
Navajo Happy Song 84
Corn Grinding Song (Zuñi) 85
Rain Dance (Zuñi) 86

COLUMBUS DAY 87
He Knew the Earth Was Round-O 88
It's All Wrong 89
My Spanish Guitar 90

HALLOWEEN 91
There Was a Li'l Woman Who
  Took a Stroll 92
Whippily, Whoppily, Whoop 93
Skeleton Bones 94
Little Ghost 95
Jack-o'-lanterns 96
Ten Little Goblins 96

ELECTION DAY 97
Ma! Ma! Where is Papa? 98
Times Are Sadly Out of Joint 99
For He's a Jolly Good Fellow 100

VETERANS DAY 101
The Marines' Hymn 102
The Caissons Go Rolling Along 103
You're in the Army Now 104
Reveille 104

THANKSGIVING DAY 105
Over the River and Thro' the Woods 106
Turkey in the Straw 107
On the First Thanksgiving Day 108

HANUKKAH 109
Hanukkah Song 110
My Dreydl 111
Rock of Ages 112

CHRISTMAS 113
The Star of Bethlehem 114
Fum, Fum, Fum! 115
Go Tell It on the Mountain 116
The Holy Child 117
O Christmas Tree 118
There Was a Donkey Standing By 119
The Twelve Days of Christmas 120
Christmas Day in the Morning 121
Jolly 'Ol' Saint Nicholas 122

BIRTHDAYS 123
Birthday Song 124

OTHER HOLIDAY SONGS TO SING 125

INDEX 127

NEW YEAR'S DAY

January 1

The joyful sounds of this holiday are heard all over the world. It is a time for parties, dancing, singing—a time when families and friends get together to welcome the New Year that begins on the first day of January.

January was named by the early Romans after Janus, their god of gates and doors. Janus was shown with two faces, one looking to the past and the other to the future. As we celebrate at the stroke of midnight that begins New Year's Day, we glance back to the year that has passed and look forward hopefully to a brighter new one as we wish each other "Happy New Year!"

Program note: In this act, Mr. Stork will fly on stage with a new baby. The management asks the audience not to wake the baby by clapping too loudly.

ACT I
Mr. Stork

Wassail Song

"Wassail," a toast for a festive occasion, comes from two words of an old English language that mean "Be healthy." In England, "wassailers" sing carols from house to house; this song expresses good wishes for the coming year.

moderately

Here we come a - was-sail-ing A - mong the leaves so green,

Here we come a - wan - d'ring, So fair — to be seen:

Chorus:

Love and joy come to you, And to you your was-sail

too, And God bless you, and send — you a Hap - py New

Year, And God send you a Hap - py New Year.

2. We are not daily beggars
   That beg from door to door,
   But we are neighbors' children
   Whom you have seen before:
            Chorus:

3. We have got a little purse
   Of stretching leather skin;
   We want a little sixpence
   To line it well within:
            Chorus:

4. God bless the master of this house,
   Likewise the mistress too,
   And all the little children
   That 'round the table go:
            Chorus:

Edited text by R. Q. _____

This old English round in three parts can also be sung on other joyous holidays throughout the year, whenever church bells ring.

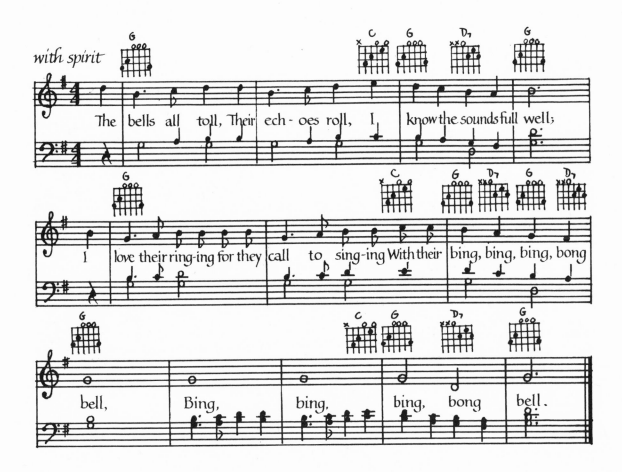

Auld Lang Syne

This song from Scotland is sung as the clock strikes twelve on New Year's Eve. Almost everyone knows the tune and the words. In fact, "Auld Lang Syne" (meaning "For Old Times' Sake"), "Happy Birthday," and "For He's a Jolly Good Fellow" are the three most popular songs of all time in the United States and many other parts of the world.

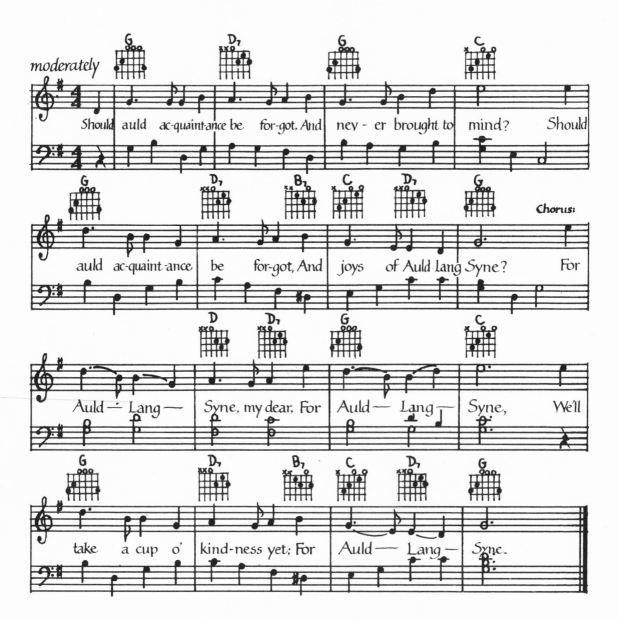

2. Give me your hand, my trusty friend,
And here's a hand of mine.
We'll take a cup o' kindness now
For Auld Lang Syne.

Chorus:

Edited text by R. Q.

DR. MARTIN LUTHER KING, JR'S BIRTHDAY

January 15

Born on January 15, 1929, Dr. Martin Luther King, Jr., won the Nobel Peace Prize in 1964 for his leadership in the field of human rights. He had worked to unite black and white Americans and to guide them in nonviolent action to achieve racial equality and freedom from discrimination.

On April 4, 1968, at the age of 39, Dr. King was killed by an assassin's bullet. But his work still lives on. Millions of people honor his memory each year on his birthdate. Recalling his love of music, they often sing some of his favorite songs in memorial services and community programs.

Program note: The management regrets that time will not permit more than twenty curtain calls for the Bird Friends.

BLACK · WHITE · TOGETHER

ACT II
The Bird Friends

We Can Overcome

This song is a variant of the very old spiritual "I Will Overcome." During the freedom marches inspired by Dr. Martin Luther King, Jr., in the 1960s, many people made up new verses to express their hopes and beliefs. Whatever words are used ("I Will," "We Shall," "We Can"), this melody is now known all over the world as a song of freedom, brotherhood, and dignity.

2. We can build a new world,
We can build a new world,
We can build a new world some day.
Oh, here in my heart
I do believe
We can build a new world some day.

3. We can walk in peace,
We can walk in peace,
We can walk in peace one day.
Oh, here in my heart
I do believe
We can walk in peace one day.

NOTE: *You may want to make up new verses of your own for this song.*

12

Edited text by R. Q.

He's Got This Whole World In His Hands

This classic spiritual is often sung in performances by famous singers. It expresses the faith that helped Dr. Martin Luther King, Jr., in his work to achieve equality for all.

2. He's got the clouds and the sky in His hands,
   He's got the moon and the sun in His hands,
   He's got the twinklin' stars in His hands,
   He's got this whole world in His hands.

3. He's got hope for us, brother, in His hands,
   He's got hope for us, sister, in His hands,
   He's got hope for us, children, in His hands,
   He's got this whole world in His hands.

4. He's got the tiny little babies in His hands,
   He's got all the little children in His hands,
   He's got the grown-up people in His hands,
   He's got this whole world in His hands.

NOTE: *You may add more verses by making up your own phrases, such as "rich and poor," "happy and sad," and others of your own invention.*

Edited text by R. Q.

Michael, Row the Boat Ashore

Here is another old spiritual that was often sung in the 1960s. It expresses the joy of working together to reach a common goal.

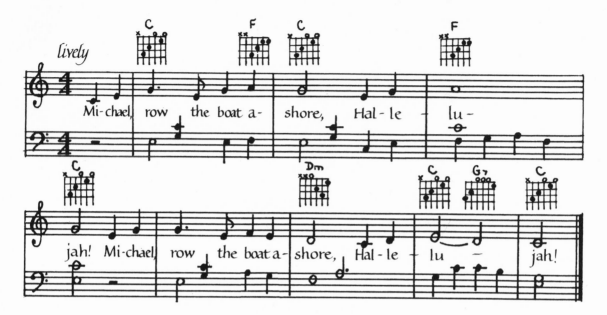

2. Brother, follow me ashore, Hallelujah!
   Sister, follow me ashore, Hallelujah!

3. Come and help to guide the boat, Hallelujah!
   Work together to stay afloat, Hallelujah!

4. Jordan's river is deep and cold, Hallelujah!
   Chills the body but not the soul, Hallelujah!

5. Trumpet, sound the jubilee, Hallelujah!
   Cross this river and we'll be free, Hallelujah!

6. Michael, row the boat ashore, Hallelujah!
   Michael, row the boat ashore, Hallelujah!

NOTE: You can make up verses to this song—anything that tells of cooperation in the quest for peace.

Edited text by R. Q.

ABRAHAM LINCOLN'S BIRTHDAY

February 12

He was called "Father Abraham" and "Honest Abe"—he was Abraham Lincoln, one of the greatest presidents of the United States, who served our country during the Civil War.

Lincoln was born on February 12, 1809, and was raised in the woods and prairies of Kentucky, Indiana, and Illinois. The story of his rise from pioneer storekeeper to president has been an inspiration to many and the theme of countless books, plays, and songs. We remember his gentle kindness, his great deeds, and his eloquent words when we celebrate his birthday.

Program note: In this act, Mr. Penguin will split some rails for a rail fence. The audience is requested to watch out for flying wood chips.

ACT III
Mr. Penguin

Lincoln and Liberty

"Lincoln and Liberty," one of Lincoln's campaign songs, is still popular today. It was written by an unknown author to the tune of "Ol' Rosin the Beau."

16

2. They'll find what by felling and mauling
   Our railmaker statesman can do:
   For the people are everywhere calling
   For Lincoln and Liberty too.
   Then up with our banner so glorious,
   The star-spangled red, white, and blue,
   We'll fight till our banner's victorious
   For Lincoln and Liberty too.

Traditional text

Lincoln heard this song for the first time in 1860 when his sons Tad and Willie repeated what the crowds were singing about him. Lincoln was then a candidate for the presidency of the United States. The tune was from a popular spiritual; you may know other words to it, such as "The Old Gray Mare" or "Here We Sit Like Birds in the Wilderness."

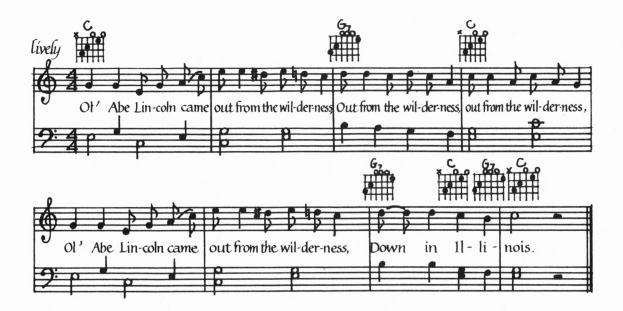

2. Ol' Abe Lincoln always spoke for our liberty,
   Spoke for our liberty, spoke for our liberty,
   Ol' Abe Lincoln always spoke for our liberty,
   Down in Illinois.

3. Ol' Abe Lincoln believed in our freedom rights,
   Believed in our freedom rights, believed in our freedom rights,
   Ol' Abe Lincoln believed in our freedom rights,
   Down in Illinois.

Edited text and additional verses by R. Q.

The Battle Hymn of the Republic

In 1861, Julia Ward Howe wrote these stirring words after hearing some soldiers sing "John Brown's Body." Even today, her immortal lyrics can move us deeply as we recall Lincoln's efforts to unify our land during the strife of civil war.

with feeling

Mine eyes have seen the glo-ry of the com-ing of the Lord; He is tramp-ling out the vin-tage where the grapes of wrath are stored; He has loosed the fate-ful light-ning of His ter-ri-ble swift sword; His truth is march-ing on.

Chorus:

Glo-ry, glo-ry! Hal-le-lu – jah! Glo-ry, glo-ry! Hal-le-lu – jah! Glo-ry, glo-ry! Hal-le-lu – jah! His truth is march-ing on.

Traditional text

VALENTINE'S DAY

February 14

There are several stories told about the origin of Valentine's Day, and no one really knows which is nearest to the truth. It may have begun with the ancient Roman custom of choosing partners by drawing names from a box, or from the feast of Saint Valentine who cured a child of blindness. In any case, today it is a time for singing love songs and giving cards decorated with lacy hearts that say "I love you."

———

Program note: Our first show-stopper will be the Swan Sisters' formation of a heart during their famous Swan Ballet.

ACT IV
The Swan Sisters

Mister Frog Went A-Courting

The earliest recorded date for this old favorite is 1549. The song comes from England and has had many variations in the United States.

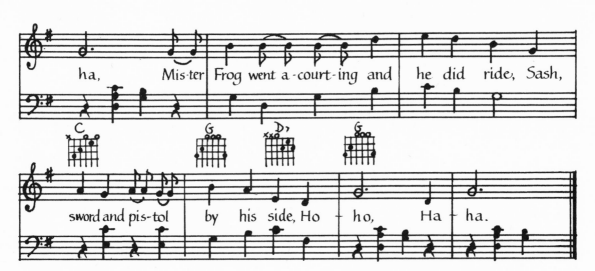

2. He rode on up to Miss Mouse's door, Ho-ho, Ha-ha,
   He rode on up to Miss Mouse's door
   Where he had been the day before, Ho-ho, Ha-ha.

3. He put Miss Mouse upon his knee, Ho-ho, Ha-ha,
   He put Miss Mouse upon his knee,
   Sayin', "Missy Mouse, please marry me," Ho-ho, Ha-ha.

4. "And where will the wedding supper be?," Ho-ho, Ha-ha,
   "And where will the wedding supper be?"
   "Down by the lake by the hollow tree," Ho-ho, Ha-ha.

5. "And what will the wedding supper be?," Ho-ho, Ha-ha,
   "And what will the wedding supper be?"
   "One black bug and one little flea," Ho-ho, Ha-ha.

6. Off they went rowing across the lake, Ho-ho, Ha-ha,
   Off they went rowing across the lake,
   And got gobbled up by a big black snake, Ho-ho, Ha-ha.

7. Before the songbook is put on the shelf, Ho-ho, Ha-ha,
   Before the songbook is put on the shelf,
   If you want a happy ending, sing it yourself, Ho-ho, Ha-ha.

Edited text by R. Q.

A Paper of Pins

This old American folk song is based on an English courtship game, "The Keys of Canterbury." It's a good song for group singing. You can make up any number of verses and endings yourself.

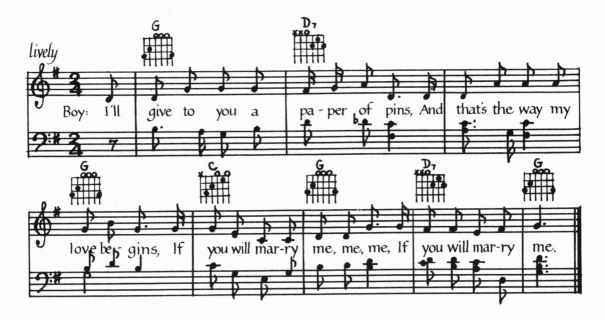

2. Girl: I'll not accept your paper of pins,
   If that's the way your love begins,
   And I'll not marry you, you, you,
   No, I'll not marry you.

3. Boy: I'll give to you a dress of red,
   Stitched all around with a golden thread,
   If you will marry me, me, me,
   If you will marry me.

4. Girl: I'll not accept your dress of red,
   All stitched around with a golden thread,
   And I'll not marry you, you, you,
   And I'll not marry you.

5. Boy: I'll give to you the keys to my chest,
   And all the money that I possess,
   If you will marry me, me, me,
   If you will marry me.

6. Girl: I will accept the keys to your chest,
   And all the money that you possess,
   Yes, I will marry you, you, you,
   Yes, I will marry you.

7. Boy: So you love coffee and I love tea;
   You love money but you don't love me.
   I won't marry you, you, you,
   No, I won't marry you.

8. Girl: Then I shall choose to be an old maid,
   And take a chair and sit in the shade,
   And I will marry none at all,
   I'll marry none at all.

If you want the boy to marry the girl, try this ending instead:

7: Boy: Oh, what is money to me without you?
   Please take my heart and my savings too,
   And I will marry you, you, you,
   And I will marry you.

Edited text by R. Q.

Love Somebody, Yes I Do

In the early 1800s, strict rules of etiquette made it hard for boys and girls to get acquainted. But at play-parties—dances similar to square dancing that were derived from children's singing games—young couples could hold hands in public without disapproval from their elders. This song is from these play-parties and it is sung today at square dances.

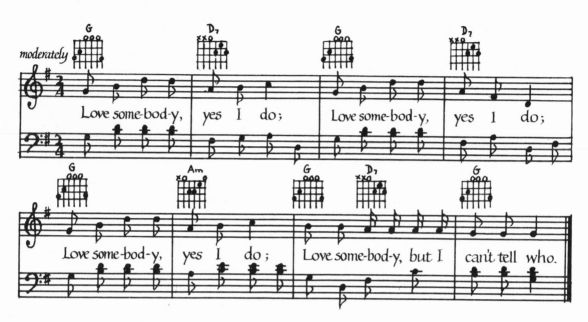

Love some-bod-y, yes I do; Love some-bod-y, yes I do;
Love some-bod-y, yes I do; Love some-bod-y, but I can't tell who.

2. Love somebody, yes I do; Love somebody, yes I do;
   Love somebody, yes I do; Hope somebody wants to love me too.

Edited text by R. Q.

Billy Boy

Based on the old English ballad "Lord Randall," this song has been played and sung in the southern mountains of the United States as far back as 1800. You can have fun making up your own verses to the music, which is found on page 95 ("Little Ghost").

1. Say, where have you been, Billy Boy, Billy Boy,
   Say, where have you been, handsome Billy?
   I went out to seek a wife and met the joy of my life,
   But she's a young thing and cannot leave her mother.

2. Did she bake a cherry pie, Billy Boy, Billy Boy,
   Did she bake a cherry pie, handsome Billy?
   Yes, she baked a cherry pie quick's a cat can wink her eye,
   But she's a young thing and cannot leave her mother.

3. And did she tell her age, Billy Boy, Billy Boy,
   And did she tell her age, handsome Billy?
   Four times six and three times sev'n, Two times forty and elev'n,
   She's a young thing and cannot leave her mother.

Edited text by R. Q.

GEORGE WASHINGTON'S BIRTHDAY

February 22 (traditional) or
the third Monday in February (Federal holiday)

George Washington's name is etched in United States history as "The Father of His Country." Born in Virginia in 1732, Washington served as Commander in Chief of the Continental Armies that won America's independence during the Revolutionary War, and was then elected the first president of the United States. The birthday of this great and strong leader was celebrated throughout the young country even during his own lifetime. Today we pay tribute each year to his bravery, his integrity, and his leadership.

Program note: In this act, Mr. Chickadee will attempt to chop down a cherry tree. The audience is advised not to worry: the Arbor Day/ Earth Day songsters will prevent this from happening.

ACT V
Mr.
Chickadee

Yankee Doodle

During the Revolutionary War, and even earlier, the British sang this song to poke fun at the Americans. But Americans enjoyed the humor of it and quickly made the song their own. This version tells of a child's first sight of George Washington at an army camp.

2. Father and I went down to camp
   Along with Captain Good'in,
   And there we saw the men and boys
   As thick as hasty puddin'.
         Chorus:

3. There was Captain Washington
   Upon a slapping stallion,
   A-giving orders to his men;
   I guess there was a million.
         Chorus:

4. There I saw a little keg,
   The heads were made of leather.
   They knocked upon it with some sticks
   To call the folks together.
         Chorus:

5. Then I saw a swamping gun
   As big as logs of maple
   Upon a mighty little cart,
   A load for Father's cattle.
         Chorus:

6. Came the time they shot it off,
   It took a horn of powder,
   And made a noise like Father's gun,
   Only a nation louder.
          Chorus:

7. Scared me so I scampered off
   Nor stopped as I remember
   Nor turned around till I got home,
   Locked safe in Mother's chamber.
          Chorus:

Edited text by R. Q. ————————————————————

This hymn, written in 1770 by William Billings, quickly became a favorite of the Minutemen and was declared the first national hymn of the United States. No one is quite sure why it is called "Chester"; perhaps it was a dedication hymn to the town of Chester, Pennsylvania—the oldest town in that state.

2. What grateful off'ring shall we bring?
   What shall we render to this Lord?
   Loud Hallelujah let us sing,
   And praise His name on ev'ry chord.

Traditional text

Washington the Great

This salute to George Washington is based on a very old folk song from Tennessee.

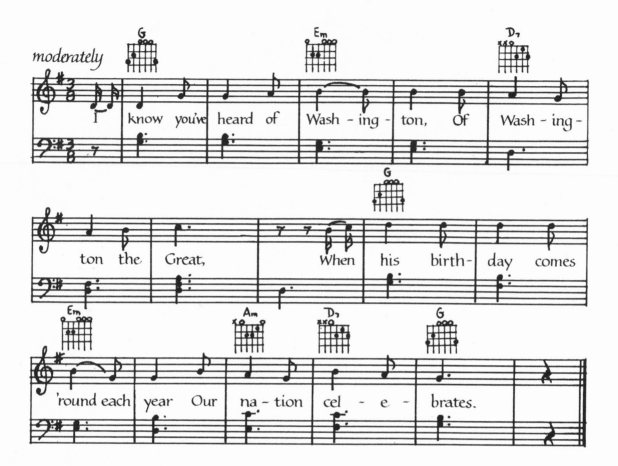

I know you've heard of Wash - ing - ton, Of Wash - ing - ton the Great, When his birth- day comes 'round each year Our na - tion cel - e - brates.

2. He became a great commander
When England ruled our land;
He was asked to lead our armies
To take a freedom stand.

3. When we won our independence
With Washington the Great,
We wanted him for President
Of the United States.

4. He has been our nation's hero
With deeds to emulate,
Like the dignity and wisdom
Of Washington the Great.

New text by R. Q.

SAINT PATRICK'S DAY

March 17

This lively holiday honors the patron saint of Ireland, who brought Christianity to the island in the 5th century. Legend says that he drove all the snakes out of Ireland. On this day, people wear shamrocks or green clothing to remind them of the Emerald Isle. All day and through the night there are parades, dinners, dances, and lots of merrymaking. To many, Saint Patrick's Day is a sign that winter is nearly over, giving the festivities an added joy!

Program note: The management will furnish free Kleenex to those who need it when Mr. Parrot sings "Cockles and Mussels."

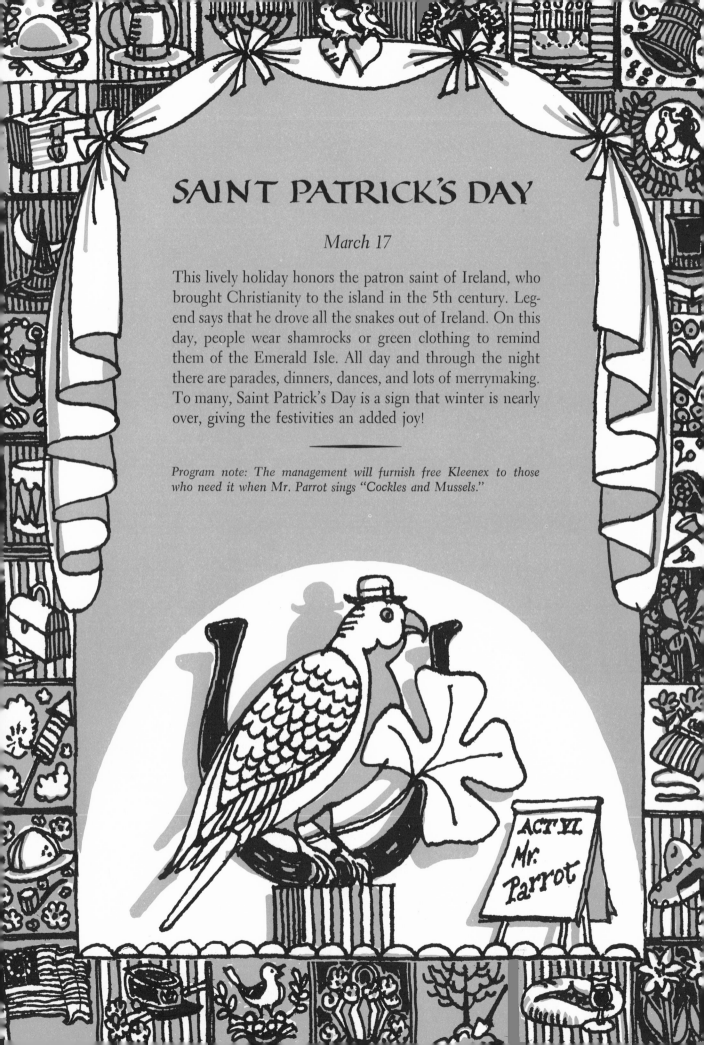

Saint Patrick Was a Gentleman

In this folk song, the Irish poke fun at themselves. The lively humor contributes to the fun and laughter of the holiday.

with spirit

Saint Pat-rick was a gen-tle-man and came from de-cent peo - ple, His church was built in Dub-lin town and up-on it was a stee - ple, His fa—ther was a Flan-ni-gan, His moth-er was a Gra-dy, His sis-ter was a Hou-li-han, and his bro-ther was a Bra-dy.

Chorus: Here's suc-cess to bold Saint Pat-rick's fist, for he's a Saint so cle - ver, He gave the toads and frogs a twist and van-ished snakes for- ev - er.

2. There's not a mile on Em'rald Isle where slimy vermin musters;
Where'er he put his foot a'ground, he wiped them out in clusters.
The frogs they hopped, the toads they plopped, kersplash into the water,
The snakes packed up their bags and fled to save themselves from slaughter.
Chorus:

28

Edited text by R. Q.

Cockles and Mussels

Along with the humorous songs that are sung on Saint Patrick's Day, sentimental and bittersweet songs are always included. Here is a classic Irish folk song in this tradition.

2. She was a fishmonger,
    Tho' sure 'twas no wonder,
    For so were her mother and father before:
    They each wheel'd their barrow
    Thro' streets broad and narrow,
        Chorus:

3. She died of a fever
    For no one could save her,
    And that was farewell to sweet Molly Malone:
    Now her ghost wheels her barrow
    Thro' streets broad and narrow,
        Chorus:

Edited text and music by R. Q.

Michael Finnegan

Comic songs based on Irish names are traditional entertainment for parties, picnics, camp cookouts, and other gatherings. "Michael Finnegan" is the all-time favorite of these Irish "name songs."

2. There was a young man named Michael Finnegan,
   He went fishing with a pin again,
   Caught a fish and dropped it in again,
   Poor, poor Michael Finnegan. Begin again!

3. There was a young man named Michael Finnegan,
   He squawked up an awful din again,
   Because of that he could not sing again,
   Poor, poor Michael Finnegan. Begin again!

4. There was a young man named Michael Finnegan,
   He grew fat and then grew thin again,
   Then he croaked and had to begin again,
   Poor, poor Michael Finnegan. CUT!

Edited text by R. Q.

APRIL FOOLS' DAY

April 1

Unless you've checked your calendar on March 31, you may find yourself caught unawares the next day by a practical joke such as: Your friend calls you and says, "Close your windows—there's a tornado coming!" When you say, "There is?," your friend will respond with a loud "APRIL FOOL!"

Formerly known as All Fools' Day, April Fools' Day has long been reserved as a time for playing harmless jokes, telling silly riddles, and singing ridiculous or nonsense songs.

Program note: Be prepared to cry during Mr. Duck's and Mr. Pigeon's act—April Fool!

ACT VII
Mr. Duck
&
Mr. Pigeon

There's a Hole in Our Bucket

As you sing this old humorous folk song, Liza should become more and more exasperated with Waldo.

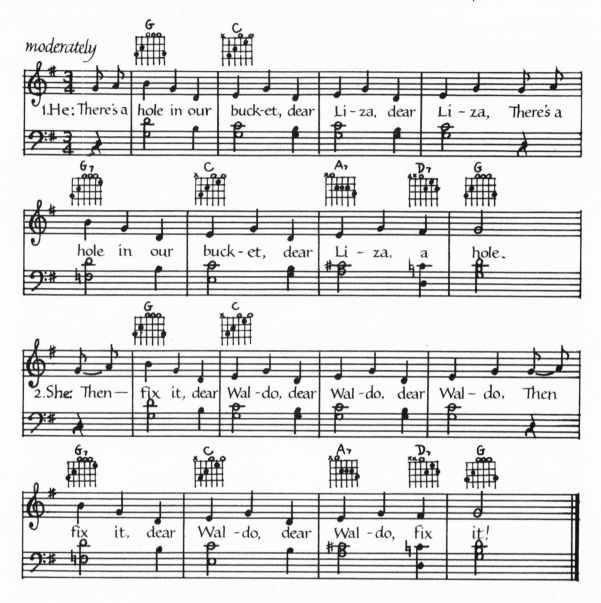

3. He: With what shall I fix it, dear Liza? . . . with what?

4. She: With straw, dear Waldo . . . with straw!

5. He: The straw is too long, dear Liza . . . too long.

6. She: Then cut it, dear Waldo . . . cut it!

7. He: With what shall I cut it, dear Liza? . . . with what?

8. She: With a knife, dear Waldo . . . a knife!

9. He: The knife is too dull, dear Liza . . . too dull.

10. She: Then sharpen it, dear Waldo . . . sharpen it!

11. He: With what shall I sharpen it, dear Liza? . . . with what?

12. She: With a stone, dear Waldo . . . a stone!

13. He: The stone is too dry, dear Liza . . . too dry.

14. She: Then wet it, dear Waldo . . . wet it!

15. He: With what shall I wet it, dear Liza? . . . with what?

16. She: With water, dear Waldo . . . with water!

17. He: In what shall I fetch it, dear Liza? . . . in what?

18. She: In a bucket, dear Waldo . . . a bucket!
19. He: THERE'S A HOLE IN OUR BUCKET, DEAR LIZA, DEAR LIZA,
       THERE'S A HOLE IN OUR BUCKET, DEAR LIZA, A HOLE.

Traditional text

There's a Flea in Lizzie's Ear

A nonsense song that is guaranteed to joggle the mind.

lively

Peep-ing through the knot-hole —— of Gram-pa's wood-en leg, ——

Who'll feed the dog when I am gone? ——

Go get the ax, —— there's a flea in Liz-zie's ear, Oh, a

boy's —— best friend is his moth-er. ——

2. I fell from a window,
   A second-story window,
   Who left their skates upon the sill?
   Go get the ax,
   There's a gnat on Lizzie's thumb,
   Oh, a boy's best friend is his mother.

3. A horsey stood around,
   With his feet upon the ground,
   Why do they build the shore so near the ocean?
   Go get the ax,
   There's a fly on Lizzie's toe,
   Oh, a boy's best friend is his mother.

Edited text by R. Q.

33

This Ol' Man

*A popular **play-party** song that is based on an old nursery rhyme.*

with spirit

This ol' man, he goes one, he goes nick-nack with a drum, With a nick-nack pad-dy whack, give the dog a bone, This ol' man goes roll-ing home.

2. This ol' man, he goes two, he goes nick-nack with a shoe,
   With a nick-nack paddy whack, give the toad a flea,
   This ol' man goes rolling home.

3. This ol' man, he goes three, he goes nick-nack with a tree,
   With a nick-nack paddy whack, give the fish a worm,
   This ol' man goes rolling home.

4. This ol' man, he goes four, he goes nick-nack with a door,
   With a nick-nack paddy whack, give the cat some cream,
   This ol' man goes rolling home.

5. This ol' man, he goes five, he goes nick-nack with a hive,
   With a nick-nack paddy whack, give the bees a sting,
   This ol' man goes rolling home.

6. This ol' man, he goes six, he goes nick-nack with a stick,
   With a nick-nack paddy whack, give the horse some oats,
   This ol' man goes rolling home.

7. This ol' man, he goes seven, he goes nick-nack with eleven,
   With a nick-nack paddy whack, eight, nine, ten alone,
   This ol' man goes rolling home.

Edited text by R. Q.

PAN-AMERICAN DAY

April 14

Pan American Day is an annual festival of parades, dances, and parties to celebrate the anniversary of the founding of the Pan American Union. The first Pan American conference was held on April 14, 1890. This official international organization was established to develop closer cooperation among the twenty-one republics of North, Central, and South America. In the United States, the celebration honors both our Latin American friends to the south, and our neighbors to the north.

Program note: During her act, Señorita Paroquet will toss tropical flowers to the audience. The audience is requested to remain seated!

Cielito Lindo

This beautiful Mexican song was sung in the United States long before California became a state. The title means "Heavenly Beauty."

with feeling

From la Sier - ra Mo-re-na, Cie - li - to Lin-do, Comes to us steal-ing, ____ Dark eyes so ____ deep, re-veal-ing, Cie-li - to Lin-do, ex - press-ing feel - ing. ____

Chorus: Ay, ay, ay, ay! ____ Sing, nev - er sor - row! ____ Our hearts are made hap-py with sing-ing, Cie-li - to Lin-do, sing ____ ne - ver sor - row! ____

SPANISH: De la Sierra Morena, Cielito Lindo, Vienen bajando, Un par de ojitos negros, Cielito Lindo, de contrabando. Chorus: Ay, ay, ay, ay! Canta y no llores, Porque cantando se alegran, Cielito Lindo, los corazones.

English version by R. Q.

Chacarera

This old Argentine folk song calls for improvised dancing while it is sung. The title means someone from a particular region, like saying that someone from New York is a "New Yorker."

softly

1. Cha-ca- re -ra, Cha-ca — re -ra, I've been told — by a hum-ming
   re -ra, Cha-ca — re -ra, I've been told — by a car-di-

bird —— That you sing with the lit- tle lark And the
nal—— That the rhyth-m of your sing-ing Makes the

sun ris — es to hear you. 2. Cha-ca- -en. 3. Cha-ca-
wheat be - gin to rip-

re-ra, Cha-ca — re-ra, sing, sing, sing with-out stop- ping That the

rhyth-m of your sweet song Will keep rip-en-ing our wheat.

SPANISH:

1. Chacarera, chacarera,
   Me ha contado un picaflor
   Que con las alondras cantas
   Y a escucharte sale el sol.

2. Chacarera, chacarera,
   Me ha contado un cardenal
   Que al compás de tus canciones
   Madurando va el trigal.

3. Chacarera, chacarera,
   Canta, canta sin cesar,
   Que al compás de tus contares
   Madurando va el trigal.

English version by R. Q.

37

La Cucaracha

"La Cucaracha" ("The Cockroach") is one of Mexico's oldest folk songs. You can make up more nonsense verses about the cockroach in Spanish or English, or both.

with spirit

La cu-ca-rach-a, La cu-ca-rach-a, Ya no quier-e cam-i-nar, Por-que no tien-e, Por-que le fal-ta, La pa-ti-ta prin-ci-pal.

ENGLISH:

1. La cucaracha, la cucaracha,
   Doesn't care to travel here,
   Because she hasn't,
   Oh, no, she hasn't,
   One of her paws at the rear.

2. La cucaracha, la cucaracha,
   Sings it loud and sings it far,
   Because she hasn't,
   Oh, no, she hasn't,
   A pick to strum her guitar.

3. La cucaracha, la cucaracha,
   Has to let her head go bare,
   Because she hasn't,
   Oh, no, she hasn't,
   A little hat she can wear.

4. La cucaracha, la cucaracha,
   Doesn't travel out at night,
   Because she hasn't,
   Oh, no, she hasn't,
   A little candle to light.

5. La cucaracha, la cucaracha,
   Often bumps into a tree,
   Because she hasn't,
   Oh, no, she hasn't,
   Glasses to help her to see.

Edited music, translation, and additional verses by R. Q.

EASTER

*The first Sunday following the
first full moon after March 22*

On Easter Sunday the resurrection of Christ is celebrated.
But Easter is also a festival of spring and hope, the renewal
of life after the chill of winter. On this holiday, beautiful
white lilies decorate churches and homes, and many people
celebrate by wearing new spring outfits.

    Other traditions of Easter are feasts, parades, and deco-
rated eggs hidden by the Easter bunny for children to find
in the morning. Families and friends often gather to ob-
serve this joyful day together.

---

*Program note: Another show-stopper will be Baby Chick's incredible
breaking out of an Easter egg. The audience is requested to be patient.*

ACT IX
Baby
Chick

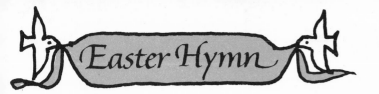

Easter Hymn

Charles Wesley, 1707-88, was a priest of the Church of England and a Methodist evangelical preacher. He composed and wrote the words to some 6500 hymns, among them "Hark! the Herald Angels Sing" and this beautiful song that is heard resounding everywhere on Easter.

2. Lives again our glorious King, Alleluia!
   Where, O death, is now thy sting? Alleluia!
   Once He died our souls to save, Alleluia!
   Where's thy victory, O grave? Alleluia!

3. Love's redeeming work is done, Alleluia!
   Fought the fight, the battle won, Alleluia!
   Death in vain forbids Him rise, Alleluia!
   Christ has opened Paradise, Alleluia!

4. Soar we now where Christ has led, Alleluia!
   Following our exalted Head, Alleluia!
   Made like Him, like Him we rise, Alleluia!
   Ours the cross, the grave, the skies, Alleluia!

Traditional text

O Glorious Bells of Easter

The stirring sounds of church bells ringing in unison on Easter morning are recreated in this song. The turn-of-the-century music was written by H. P. Danks, but the author of the lyrics is unknown.

2. O glorious bells of Easter Day!
   Ding dong ding dong ding dong ding dong!
   The hills that rise up to the skies
   All echo with your word,
   Ding dong ding dong ding dong!
   The skies resound your glorious sound,
   The rising of the Lord,
   The rising of the Lord!

Edited text and music by R. Q.

Easter Basket

A children's Easter song that poses a question at the end: Is there really an Easter Bunny?

A bas - ket! A bas - ket! I found a lit -tle bas - ket! I found it un - der -neath my bed, I won - der how it got there?

2. It's Easter! It's Easter! I know that it is Easter.
   Just look at all the colored eggs
   And candy in my basket!

3. A bunny! A bunny! I know a bunny left it;
   For who could crawl beneath my bed
   Unless it was a bunny?

4. He likes me! He likes me! I know that bunny likes me;
   For here's a chocolate Easter egg
   And jelly beans to chew on!

5. I know it! I know it! I know the bunny left it;
   For here's a note addressed to me,
   It says, "Love from the Bunny!"

Spoken at the end: SINCE WHEN COULD BUNNIES WRITE?

Text by R. Q.

Itisket, Itasket

This is a variation of the well-known nursery song with the same music as "Easter Basket."

Itisket, Itasket, A red and yellow basket;
I went to take it to a friend,
But on my way I lost it.

NOTE: *Make up other words to this song to tell how the basket was found.*

Text by R. Q.

PASSOVER

*Begins on the 14th day of the Hebrew month
of Nisan (around the same time as Easter)*

The holiday of Passover lasts for eight days. It begins with a joyful night of feasting with family and friends. At this feast, called a Seder, the youngest child in the family asks, "Why is this night different from all other nights?" Then the head of the family explains that Passover celebrates Moses' leading of the Jews out of slavery in Egypt to a land of freedom. It is a time for remembering the past and rejoicing in the present.

Program note: In this act Mr. Owl and his son will reveal Mrs. Owl's secret recipe for haroseth—with Mrs. Owl's permission, of course!

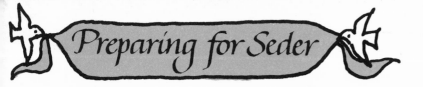
What better way to tell what happens at a Seder feast than to sing this song?

moderately

Come, Je - re - my, E - tan! Put these big white a - prons on!

Boys, too, must work to -day, Help-ing Grand-ma in ev'-ry way,

So that by to - night, — Se-der ta - ble will look right,

Each thing shin-ing in its place, From Kid -dush thro' grace.

2. Crisp matzos first we set Underneath the coverlet.
   Next, says the Haggadah, Comes peri haadamah.
   Make haroseth tasty, Chop it fine and pasty.
   Bitter herbs and roasted bone, Elijah's cup stands all alone.

3. Bring out the Pesach wine In bottles sealed in Palestine.
   Pillows on which to lean, Candlesticks complete the scene.
   Haggadah at ev'ry plate, Now we're ready to celebrate.
   One more minute to review Mah nishtannah, then we're thro'!

Haggadah: a prayer book
haroseth: a mixture of chopped nuts, apples,
   cinnamon, and wine
Kiddush: a prayer toast

Mah nishtannah: the first words of the questions
   asked at the Seder
matzos: unleavened bread
peri haadamah: fruit that comes from the ground

See ACKNOWLEDGMENTS

Go Down, Moses

This spiritual is based on a story from the Old Testament and is most appropriate for Passover.

2. Moses took them from bondage toil,
   Let my people go!
   He led them all to freedom's soil,
   Let my people go!
          Chorus:

3. The Lord told Moses what to do,
   Let my people go!
   To take them out and see them thro',
   Let my people go!
          Chorus:

Edited text by R. Q.

Dayenu
(For That Alone We Should Be Grateful)

This ancient Hebrew folk song is one of the most traditional of the Passover songs sung at the Seder.

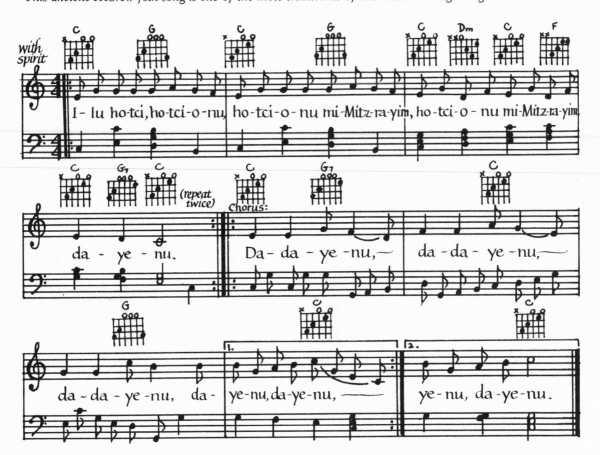

2. I-lu no-śan lo-nu es ha-Sha-both, da-ye-nu:
   I-lu no-san lo-nu es ha-Sha-both, da-ye-nu:
   Chorus:

3. I-lu no-san lo-nu es ha-To-roh, da-ye-nu:
   I-lu no-san lo-nu es ha-To-roh, da-ye-nu:
   Chorus:

4. I-lu hih-ni-so-nu l'E-retz Yis-ro-el, da-ye-nu:
   I-lu hih-ni-so-nu l'E-retz Yis-ro-el, da-ye-nu:
   Chorus:

TRANSLATION:
1. Had He (Moses) done nothing more than take us out of Egypt,
   for that alone we should be grateful!
2. Had He given us the Sabbath and nothing more, for that
   alone we should be grateful!
3. Had He given us the Torah and nothing more, for that alone
   we should be grateful!
4. Had He brought us into the land of Israel and nothing more,
   for that alone we should be grateful!

46   Traditional text

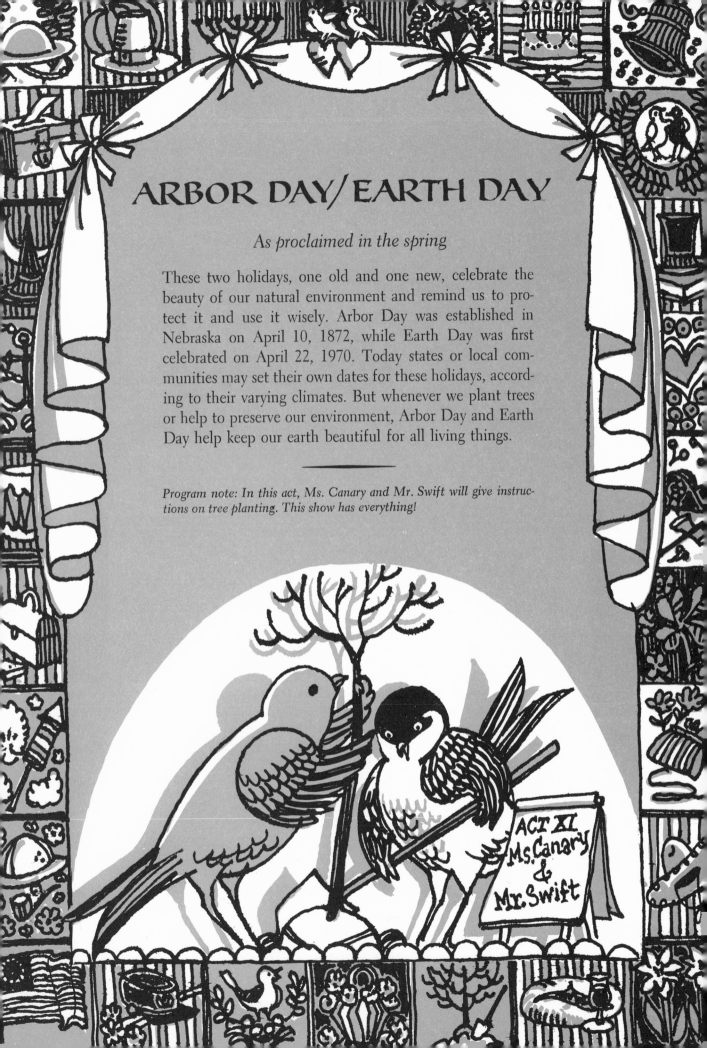

ARBOR DAY/EARTH DAY

As proclaimed in the spring

These two holidays, one old and one new, celebrate the beauty of our natural environment and remind us to protect it and use it wisely. Arbor Day was established in Nebraska on April 10, 1872, while Earth Day was first celebrated on April 22, 1970. Today states or local communities may set their own dates for these holidays, according to their varying climates. But whenever we plant trees or help to preserve our environment, Arbor Day and Earth Day help keep our earth beautiful for all living things.

Program note: In this act, Ms. Canary and Mr. Swift will give instructions on tree planting. This show has everything!

ACT XI
Ms.Canary
&
Mr.Swift

Deep in the Woods

All over the world, this very old folk song has been sung in many versions and many languages. It reminds us that all living things are dependent on one another.

with spirit

Deep in the woods there was a hill, The sweet – est hill you ev – er did see; And the hill was in the woods, (#2 – #10)

And the tall grass grew all a- round, 'round, 'round, and the tall grass grew all a – round.

✳ Note: Repeat measure for verses #2,3,4,5,6,7,8,9,10.

2. And on this hill there was a tree,
   The sweetest tree you ever did see;
   And the tree was on the hill,
   And the hill was in the woods,
   And the tall grass grew all around, 'round, 'round,
   And the tall grass grew all around.

3. And on this tree there was a limb, (etc.)
4. And on this limb there was a branch, (etc.)
5. And on this branch there was a nest, (etc.)
6. And in this nest there was an egg, (etc.)
7. And on this egg there was a bird, (etc.)
8. And on this bird there was some down, (etc.)
9. And from this down there came a quilt, (etc.)

10. And in this quilt there lay a girl,
    The sweetest girl you ever did see;
    And the girl lay in the quilt,
    And the quilt came from the down,
    And the down came from the bird,
    And the bird was on the egg,
    And the egg was in the nest,
    And the nest was on the branch,
    And the branch was on the limb,
    And the limb was on the tree,
    And the tree was on the hill,
    And the hill was in the woods,
    And the tall grass grew all around, 'round, 'round,
    And the tall grass grew all around.

48

Edited text by R. Q.

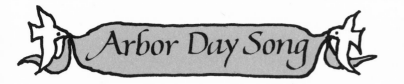

Arbor Day Song

This Israeli folk song celebrates Arbor Day, which comes much earlier in the year in Israel than it does in the United States. Sing it in harmony by repeating the first two measures of the song over and over as a chant, using "la."

It's the Same the Whole World Over

On Earth Day, people think about finding ways to keep our air fresh, our skies clean, and our waters pure. This song is a plea to join hands in the fight against pollution.

with strong feeling

It's the same the whole world o - ver,— Pol-lu - tion cov - ers our land.— Some say it is - n't a prob—lem — and won't lend a help - ing hand.— Oth-ers -ry - thing right.

2. Others try to make the effort
   To keep our parks clean and neat.
   They stop polluting our rivers
   And keep litter off the street.

3. It's a problem that we all share;
   How can we join in the fight?
   Let's start to celebrate Earth Day
   And help set everything right.

Edited music and new text by R. Q.

MAY DAY

May 1

As far back as the early Romans, a festive welcome to the month of May has been an important festival. In medieval England May Day was celebrated with games, sport, and morris dancing. Later, Robin Hood and Maid Marian came to preside as Lord and Lady of the May, and by the 16th century the holiday was known as Robin Hood's Day, with Robin Hood plays as part of the festivities.

In the United States up until the 1930s, May Day was an occasion for carol singing, dances around the Maypole, and gifts of flowers to each household. Although the holiday is no longer celebrated widely, some of its lovely traditions have stayed with us. You might secretly leave a basket of flowers on someone's doorstep on May Day morning.

Program note: In this act Ms. Meadowlark will demonstrate how to make May baskets. The audience is advised to provide its own flowers.

Three Little Girls

This song is based on a Mother Goose nursery rhyme; it can be sung while dancing around a Maypole.

2. The ice was thin, they all fell in,
   They all fell in, they all fell in.
   The ice was thin, they all fell in,
   So early on the first of May.
              Chorus:

3. And when they fell in they got soaking wet,
   They got soaking wet, they got soaking wet.
   And when they fell in they got soaking wet,
   And they missed the May Day party.
              Chorus:

4. Here we go dancing 'round the Maypole,
   'Round the Maypole, 'round the Maypole.
   Here we go dancing 'round the Maypole,
   The little girls had to stay home.
   Chorus:

Edited text and
additional verses by R. Q.

Now Is the Month of Maying

Thomas Morley, 1557-1603, an English composer best known for his settings of Shakespeare's songs, wrote this traditional May Day melody and lyrics.

Today's the First of May

Wouldn't it be fun to hear a secret admirer singing this song on May Day as he or she leaves a basket of flowers at your doorstep?

joyfully

To-day's the first of May,   To - day's the first of May, May, May, To-

day's the first of May,   The hap-py month of May.   So

long to you, my friend,   We'll meet a -gain, you can de -pend, We'll

meet a -gain some- day,   One hap-py day in May.

2. I leave this gift for you,
   I leave this gift for you, you, you,
   I leave this gift for you,
   May flowers just for you.
   It only is your due,
   This gift from one who loves you true,
   We'll meet again someday,
   One happy day in May.

Edited text and additional verse by R. Q.

MOTHER'S DAY

The second Sunday in May

Mother's Day was established in 1908 by Anna Jarvis, in honor of her own mother. The idea appealed to many people, and by 1914 the second Sunday in May was designated as Mother's Day by presidential proclamation.

Since then, the struggle for equal rights has opened up many new and challenging opportunities for women. But the meaning of Mother's Day has not changed, as children of all ages show their love and respect for their mothers on this joyful family holiday.

Program note: In this act, Mrs. Robin will warm her eggs. Quiet is requested during this period.

ACT XIII
Mrs. Robin

Mary

Many of the old songs written in honor of "Mother" sound very silly and sentimental today. But this song, adapted from one written by George M. Cohan in 1905, has survived the test of time. Try performing the first verse as a solo and the second with the whole group.

slow to moderate

Her name is Ma – ry, Ma – ry, plain as a – ny name can be; But with pro – pri – e – ty, so – ci – e – ty will say Ma – rie; But it was Ma – ry, Ma – ry, long be – fore the fash – ions came, And there is some – thing there that sounds so fair, It's my moth – er's name.

2. For it is Mary, Mary, plain as any name can be;
   But with propriety, society will say Marie;
   But it was Mary, Mary, long before the fashions came,
   And it's a name so dear, I love to hear,
   It's my mother's name.

56

Edited text by R. Q.

Mama's Gonna Buy

This lively new version of an old favorite brings the song up to date for a modern mother!

2. If that diamond ring is fake,
   Mama's gonna buy me an ice cream cake.

3. If that ice cream cake won't set,
   Mama's gonna buy me a clarinet.

4. If that clarinet won't toot,
   Mama's gonna buy me a swimming suit.

5. If that swimming suit don't fit,
   Mama's gonna say, "Oh, heck, I quit!"

New text by R. Q.

Hush, Little Baby

These traditional words, sung softly at a slower tempo, evoke the warmth of a mother's lullabye.

1. Hush, little baby, don't say a word,
   Mama's gonna buy you a mockingbird.

2. If that mockingbird don't sing,
   Mama's gonna buy you a diamond ring.

3. If that diamond ring turns to brass,
   Mama's gonna buy you a looking glass.

4. If that looking glass gets broke,
   Mama's gonna buy you a billy goat.

5. If that billy goat falls down,
   You'll still be the sweetest little baby in town.

Traditional text

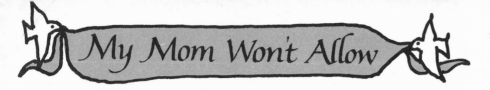

My Mom Won't Allow

This country classic is a favorite at group songfests, as each singer makes up a verse to tell what else "Mom Won't Allow." Its comedy and good humor are great fun at a lively family party on Mother's Day. Try inventing your own verses—perhaps about rock and roll music on your radio?

2. My Mom won't allow no guitar pickin' 'round here.
   My Mom won't allow no guitar pickin' 'round here.
   But I don't care what my Mom won't allow,
   Gonna pick my guitar anyhow.
   My Mom won't allow no guitar pickin' 'round here.

3. My Mom won't allow no banjo strummin' 'round here.
   My Mom won't allow no banjo strummin' 'round here.
   But I don't care what my Mom won't allow,
   Gonna plunk my banjo anyhow.
   My Mom won't allow no banjo strummin' 'round here.

Edited text by R. Q.

MEMORIAL DAY

The last Monday in May

Memorial Day, or Decoration Day as it is sometimes called, began as a patriotic holiday to honor the memory of those who died in the Civil War. Since then, it has become a day to pay tribute to the dead of all our wars.

On this day, people place flowers on gravesites and attend military ceremonies and memorial concerts. Many of the concert songs date from the Civil War, and they have been sung by soldiers in every war since then.

Program note: During their act, the Wren Brothers will demonstrate some marching formations. Volunteers from the audience may participate.

Tenting on the Old Camp Ground

Walter Kittredge, a concert ballad singer from New Hampshire, wrote these words and music during the Civil War. It became one of the most popular songs of both the North and the South.

slowly

We're tent-ing to-night on the old camp ground, Give us a song to

cheer Our wear-y hearts, a song of home, And friends we love so dear.

Chorus:

Man-y are the hearts that are wear-y to-night, Wish-ing for the war to

cease, Man-y are the hearts look-ing for the right To see the dawn of

peace. Tent-ing to-night, Tent-ing to-night, Tent-ing on the old camp ground.—

Traditional text

When Johnny Comes Marching Home Again

This song by Patrick Gilmore was also one of the most popular songs of the Civil War. It was sung with the hope that loved ones would return home safely from battle.

2. The old church bell will peal with joy, Hurrah! Hurrah!
   To welcome home our darling boy, Hurrah! Hurrah!
   The village lads and lassies say With roses they will strew the way,
   And we'll all feel joy when Johnny comes marching home.

Traditional text

Taps

The melody of this song is the bugle call played at military funerals and Memorial Day services, as well as at the close of day.

Day is done, Gone the sun, From the lake, From the hills, From the sky. All is well, Safe-ly rest, God is nigh.

2. Fading light dims the sight,
   And a star gems the sky,
   Glowing bright.
   From afar, drawing nigh,
   Falls the night.

Traditional text

Tramp! Tramp! Tramp!

This chorus of a song written by George F. Root during the Civil War tells of a prisoner's hope of rescue. It has been a popular marching song for over a century.

Tramp, tramp, tramp! the boys are march-ing, Cheer up, com-rades, they will come, And be-neath the star-ry flag We shall breathe the air a-gain Of the free land in our own be-lov-ed home

62

Traditional text

FLAG DAY

June 14

Every year on June 14, Americans honor their flag at parades and concerts, for it was on June 14, 1777, that the first official flag of the United States was adopted.

Today's Stars and Stripes is different from that first flag. The number of stars on the blue field has grown from the original thirteen, each new star representing a new state in the Union. However, the thirteen alternating red and white stripes remain just as they were on the first flag. They remind us of the thirteen colonies that joined together to form the Union.

Program note: In this act the Sparrow Brothers will hoist a flag. The audience is requested to stand at attention.

ACT XV
The Sparrow Brothers

The Star-Spangled Banner

Patriotism and love for the flag resound in every line of Francis Scott Key's lyrics for our national anthem.

Traditional text

The Red, White, and Blue

This stirring march, written in 1843, is played and sung on most patriotic occasions.

with pride

O Co-lum-bia, the gem of the o-cean, The home of the brave and the free,— The shrine of each pat-riot's de-vo-tion, A — world of-fers hom-age to thee. Thy man-dates make he-roes as-sem-ble, When Lib-er-ty's form stands in view; Thy ban-ners make ty-ran-ny trem-ble When borne by the red, white and blue;

Chorus:

When borne by the red, white and blue, When borne by the red, white and blue, Thy ban-ners make ty-ran-ny trem-ble When borne by the red, white and blue.

Repeat chorus: Three cheers for the red, white, and blue, Three cheers for the red, white, and blue, The army and navy forever, Three cheers for the red, white, and blue.

Traditional text

You're a Grand Old Flag

This popular favorite is based on a song from George M. Cohan's turn-of-the-century musical, "George Washington, Jr."

with spirit

You're a grand old flag, You're our Star-Span-gled flag, And for-e—ver in peace may you wave. You're the em-blem of the land I love, The home of the free and the brave. Ev-'ry heart beats true un-der Red, White and Blue Where there's ne-ver a boast or brag; But should auld ac-quain-tance be for-got, Keep your eye on the grand old flag.

Edited text by R. Q.

FATHER'S DAY

The third Sunday in June

Like Mother's Day, Father's Day is a time when families gather with feelings of love, this time for fathers and grand-fathers.

In 1910, Mrs. John Bruce Dodd of Spokane, Washington, organized the first celebration of Father's Day in her home town. The idea spread quickly, and in 1916, two years after the similar holiday in honor of mothers, Father's Day was proclaimed by President Woodrow Wilson. But it was not until 1972 that Father's Day became a permanently established annual holiday.

Program note: In this act, Mr. Peacock will display his full plumage —a rare treat!

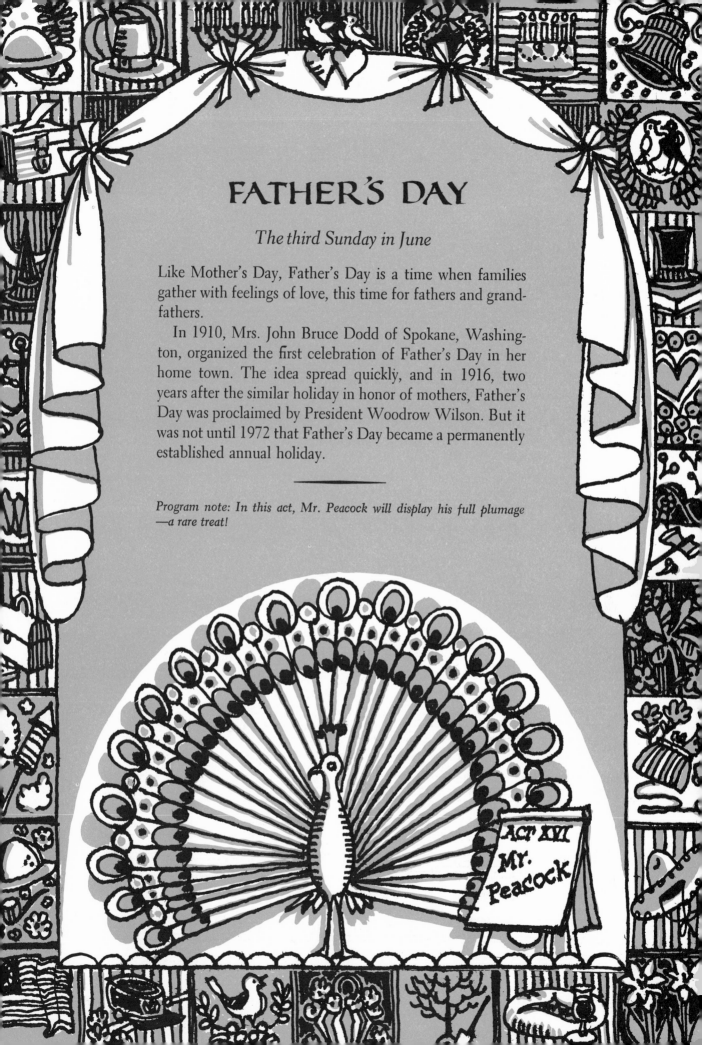

Daddy Wouldn't Buy Me a Bow Wow

Try singing this 1892 song, written and composed by Joseph Trabar, in vaudeville style.

I love my lit-tle cat, I do, With soft black silk-y hair; It comes each day with me to school And sits up-on the chair; When teach-er says,"Why do you bring that lit-tle pet of yours?", I tell her that I bring my cat A-long with me be-cause.......

Chorus:

Dad-dy would-n't buy me a bow-wow! Bow-wow! Dad-dy would-n't buy me a bow-wow! Bow-wow! I've got a lit-tle cat, And I'm ve-ry fond of that, but I'd

NOTE: *You can make up other things "Daddy Wouldn't Buy"*
and sing them to the notes of the chorus, such as:

Daddy wouldn't buy me a Batman! Batman!
Daddy wouldn't buy me a Batman! Batman!
I've got a Captain Kirk, And he's always fun to work,
But I'd rather have a Batman, man, man, man, man, etc.

Edited text by R. Q. _____

Watching for Pa

Based on Henry Clay Work's turn-of-the-century song, here is a loving homecoming welcome for Father.

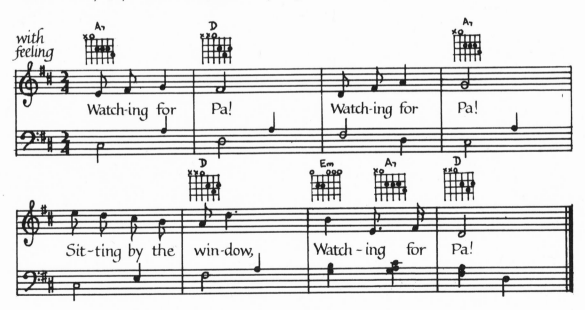

2. Waiting for Pa!
   Waiting for Pa!
   Sitting by the window,
   Waiting for Pa!

3. List'ning for Pa!
   List'ning for Pa!
   Putting in his latchkey,
   List'ning for Pa!

4. Welcoming Pa!
   Welcoming Pa!
   Running to the doorway,
   Welcoming Pa!

Additional verses by R. Q.

Daddy's Whiskers (1)

It's fun to write your own verses for this song to tell what happens to your daddy's whiskers. The first version here is for the father who likes a clean shave, and the second version is for the father who likes to grow a beard.

lively

We have a dear ol' dad-dy, We love him ev'-ry day. He has a set of whis-kers, They're al-ways in his way. Oh, they're al-ways in his way, Our horse eats them for hay, They grow in haste to dad-dy's waist, They're al-ways in his way.

Chorus:

2. Our daddy tried to shave them,
   They grew right back that day.
   He shaved them with a mower,
   They grew back anyway.
   Chorus:

3. Our daddy went out chopping,
   He struck a mighty blow.
   It didn't stop his whiskers,
   It helped to make them grow.
   Chorus:

4. Our daddy tried to blast them,
   He bought some T.N.T.
   The blasting didn't help him,
   They grew right back, you see.
   Chorus:

New text by R. Q.

Daddy's Whiskers (2)

1. We have a dear ol' daddy
   We love so much each day.
   He has a set of whiskers,
   They're never in his way.

        Chorus:

   Oh, they're never in his way,
   He likes the way they lay.
   They hide the dirt on daddy's shirt,
   They're never in his way.

2. Our daddy had a huge chest,
   But now it's all caved in.
   His whiskers got so heavy,
   He walks upon his chin.
        Chorus:

4. We have a little kitten,
   She's fun to watch at play.
   She climbs up father's whiskers
   And braids them all the way.
        Chorus:

3. We have a dear ol' mother,
   She likes the whiskers, too.
   She uses them for dusting
   And cleaning out the flue.
        Chorus:

New text by R. Q.

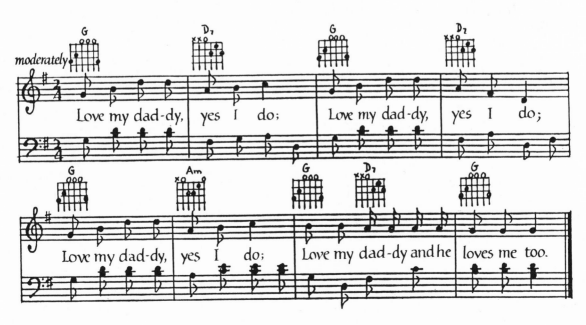
Love My Daddy, Yes I Do

Another version of "Love Somebody, Yes I Do," just for fathers.

moderately

Love my dad-dy, yes I do; Love my dad-dy, yes I do;

Love my dad-dy, yes I do; Love my dad-dy and he loves me too.

Traditional text

The No, No, Yes, Yes Aria

A special song to the tune of "Reveille" for fathers to sing in reply to: "Will you buy me?," "Can I go?," and all the countless other questions a father is asked each day.

Or if he chooses, Father may sing the aria this way (it depends on how he is asked):

Yes, yes, yes, yes, yes, yes, yes, yes, yes, yes, yes, yes, yes,
yes, yes, yes, yes, yes, yes, yes, yes, yes, yes, yes, yes, yes,
yes, yes, yes, yes, yes, yes, yes, yes, yes, yes, yes, yes, yes,
yes, yes, yes, yes, yes, yes, yes, yes, yes, yes, yes, yes, yes,
yes, yes, yes, yes, yes, yes, yes, yes, yes, yes, yes!

INDEPENDENCE DAY

July 4

On July 4, 1776, the Continental Congress adopted the Declaration of Independence. Therefore, Independence Day is a celebration of the birthday of the United States of America.

The Glorious Fourth, as orators often call it, is celebrated during the day with parades, speeches, flag waving, and bell ringing. And at night there are outdoor concerts of patriotic music and brilliant fireworks to light up the sky. In all these ways we salute the founders of our nation and remind ourselves of the goals they hoped to achieve.

Program note: In this act Mr. Eagle will leap in the nick of time from an exploding firecracker. Members of the audience are advised to cover their ears.

ACT XVII
Mr. Eagle

America the Beautiful

In 1893, an awesome view from the summit of Pike's Peak in Colorado inspired Katharine Lee Bates to write these words that were set to Samuel A. Ward's music. The verses were first published on July 4, 1895.

2. O beautiful for pilgrim feet Whose stern impassioned stress
   A thoroughfare for freedom beat Across the wilderness.
   America! America! God mend thine ev'ry flaw,
   Confirm thy soul in self-control, Thy liberty in law.

3. O beautiful for heroes prov'd In liberating strife,
   Who more than self their country loved, And mercy more than life.
   America! America! May God thy gold refine
   Till all success be nobleness And ev'ry gain divine.

4. O beautiful for patriot dreams That see beyond the years
   Thine alabaster cities gleam, Undimmed by human tears.
   America! America! God shed His grace on thee,
   And crown thy good with brotherhood From sea to shining sea.

Traditional text

Yankee Doodle Boy

*Based on a song by George M. Cohan,
this traditional favorite is good for solo
and group singing.*

America

Samuel Francis Smith, a minister, wrote these words for a service at the Park Street Church in Boston on July 4, 1831. He did not realize that the tune is Britain's national anthem, "God Save the King"! Even so, "America" was a prime candidate for the national anthem of the United States before "The Star-Spangled Banner" was officially adopted in 1931.

2. My native country thee, Land of the noble free,
   Thy name I love; I love thy rocks and rills,
   Thy woods and templed hills; My heart with rapture thrills,
   Like that above.

3. Let music swell the breeze, And ring from all the trees,
   Sweet freedom's song; Let mortal tongues awake,
   Let all that breathe partake, Let rocks their silence break,
   The sound prolong.

4. Our fathers' God, to Thee, Author of liberty,
   To Thee we sing! Long may our land be bright
   With freedom's holy light; Protect us by Thy might,
   Great God, our King!

Traditional text

LABOR DAY

The first Monday in September

In 1882, Labor Day was proposed as a holiday to honor workers, and a parade was held in New York City. It became a national holiday in 1894, saluting labor's contribution to our society.

Today Labor Day is a holiday not only for people in the labor movement but for *all* people who work: teachers, farmers, taxi drivers, doctors, salespeople, artists—everyone. On this day, people watch parades, go on picnics, attend sports events, and enjoy a day off with family and friends.

Program note: In this act, Mr. Robin will show how he works at catching worms. Fishermen take note!

Erie Canal

Canal barges, pulled by mules walking along the banks, were once the main means of transport in the northeastern United States.

moderately

I've got a mule, her name is Sal, Fif-teen miles on the E-rie Can-al. — She's a good old work-er and a good old pal, Fif-teen miles on the E-rie Can-al. — We've hauled some bar-ges in our day, Filled with lum - ber, coal and hay, And ev'-ry inch of the way we — know From Al-ba-ny — to — Buf-fa-lo. — Chorus: Low bridge ev'-ry-bo-dy down! Low bridge, for we're com-in' thro' a town! And you'll al - ways know your neigh-bor, You'll al - ways know your pal, If you've ev-er nav-i-gat-ed on the E - rie Can-al. —

2. We'd better step along, old gal,
   Fifteen miles on the Erie Canal.
   'Cause you bet your life I wouldn't part with Sal,
   Fifteen miles on the Erie Canal.
   Git up there, Sal, here comes a lock,
   We'll make Rome 'bout six o'clock,
   Just one more trip and back we'll go,
   Right back home to Buffalo.
                            Chorus:

Edited text by R. Q. ——————————————————————————

Blow the Man Down

The swinging rhythm of this old sailor chantey is that of sailors at work on the deck. The Black Ball Line was a fleet of ships, and "Kicking Jack" Williams was one of its captains.

Come all ye young fel-lows that fol-low the sea, With a yo - ho! Blow the man down! And please, pay at - ten - tion and lis - ten to me, Give me some time to blow the man down.

2. On board a Black Baller I first served my time,
   With a yo-ho! Blow the man down!
   And on the Black Baller I wasted my prime,
   Give me some time to blow the man down.

3. 'Tis larboard and starboard, you jump to the call,
   With a yo-ho! Blow the man down!
   For "Kicking Jack" Williams commands the Black Ball,
   Give me some time to blow the man down.

Edited text by R. Q.

I've Been Working on the Railroad

This song was sung by workers when the great railroads were being built across America.

80

Traditional text

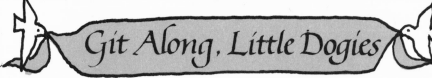

Git Along, Little Dogies

As far back as frontier days, cowboys working on the range rounding up "dogies" (yearling cattle) have sung this song.

2. So early in spring when we round up the dogies, We mark 'em and brand 'em and bob off their tails,
   And round up our horses and load the chuck wagon; We then throw the dogies out onto the trail. Chorus:

Edited text by R. Q.

Down the River

This old work song recalls the great flatboats that drifted down rivers, carrying cargo into new territories.

snappily

The riv-er is deep and the chan-nel is wide, The winds are stead-y and fair. — Oh, won't we have a snap-py good time, As we go mov-ing a-long.

Chorus:

Down the riv-er, O, down the riv-er, Hi, Down the riv-er we go, Hi-O, Down the riv-er, O, down the riv-er, Hi, down the O - HI - O!

2. The river is deep, and the channel is wide,
   The winds are steady and fair.
   Oh, Dinah, get the hoecakes done,
   As we go moving along.
   Chorus:

3. The river is deep, and the channel is wide,
   The winds are steady and fair.
   The waves they splash from shore to shore,
   As we go moving along.
   Chorus:

Edited text by R. Q.

AMERICAN INDIAN DAY

As *proclaimed*

In 1916, New York was the first state to proclaim a holiday called American Indian Day. Many other states now have this holiday on different dates throughout the year.

When we celebrate this holiday, we honor the many different cultures of America's original inhabitants, who lived on America's soil long before the Europeans arrived. It is a day to salute the American Indians' contribution to our national heritage in song, literature, dance, and magnificent works of art.

———————

Program note: In this act, Brave Hawk will demonstrate the art of Indian drum playing. We told you this show has everything!

ACT XIX
Brave
Hawk

Sioux Night Song

This song was collected in 1845 by an Indian named Thomas Commuck.

✳ Sing throughout to the tone produced by saying "Ha" through the nose, and as throaty as possible.

Traditional

Navajo Happy Song

In this song for joyous occasions, the words mean something like "tra la la." The last "yah" is shouted.

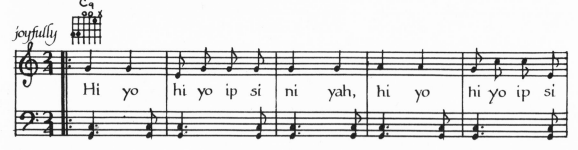

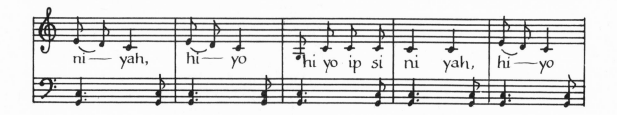

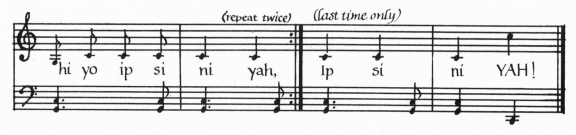

See ACKNOWLEDGMENTS

Corn-Grinding Song (Zuñi)

This Zuñi Indian song is to be sung three times; the last "HI-YE YE!" is shouted at the end.

Rain Dance (Zuñi)

This is the chorus from the great rain dance of the Zuñi Indians of New Mexico.

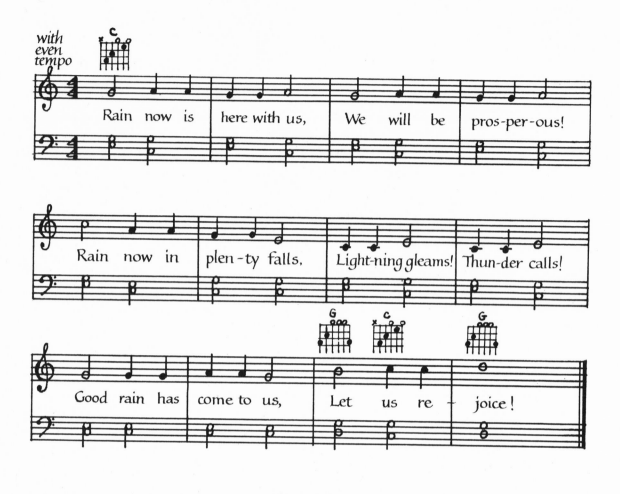

with even tempo

Rain now is here with us, We will be pros-per-ous!

Rain now in plen-ty falls, Light-ning gleams! Thun-der calls!

Good rain has come to us, Let us re - joice!

OTHER SONGS TO SING: There are, of course, many more songs of American Indian origin from the many different tribes that have lived in the United States, Canada, and Latin America. A large selection may be found at your local libraries and museums.

86

Edited by R. Q.

COLUMBUS DAY

*October 12 (traditional) or the second
Monday in October (Federal holiday)*

In many parts of North and South America, Columbus Day is celebrated with parades and cultural programs in honor of Columbus's arrival in the New World on October 12, 1492. The first observance of this holiday was held in New York City on October 12, 1792, and it became a national holiday one hundred years later.

Columbus made his first landing on an island in the Bahamas, which he named San Salvador. Columbus didn't know he had found a vast body of land that Europeans had never heard of. He believed that he had reached the Indies by a westward route, so he called the people Indians and their islands the West Indies. These names have been with us ever since.

---

*Program note: In this act, Mr. Gull will give some tips on **sailing**. The audience may submit questions for the question-and-answer period.*

ACT XX
Mr. Gull

He Knew the Earth Was Round-o

This song was written and composed in 1893 by Francis J. Bryant and has appeared in many versions.

quickly

I'll sing to you a-bout a man whose name you'll find in hist-ry, Whose

ships were the Nin - a, the Pin-ta, and the San-ta Mar-ie, All

na-vi-ga-tors young and old gave way to him quite fit-ly, His

name it was Co-lum-bus, and he came from sun-ny It - 'ly.

Chorus:

He knew the Earth was round—o! That land it could be

found—o! That cap-ti-va-ting, nav-i-ga-ting Chris-to-fo Co-lum-bo.

2. In fourteen hundred and ninety-two, 'twas then Columbus started
   From Palos on the coast of Spain, and westward he departed;
   His object was to find a route, a short one to East Indies,
   Columbus was determined tho' the wind it blew quite windy.
                                                     Chorus:

3. When sixty days away from land upon the broad Atlantic,
   His sailors became quite frightened and they nearly caused a panic,
   But after ninety days had passed, they soon discovered these shores,
   And quickly made a landing on the Isle of Salvador.
                                                     Chorus:

Edited text by R. Q. _____

For a completely silly addition to your Columbus Day singing, try this old-time music hall song.

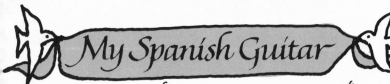

My Spanish Guitar

This humorous song is about a mythical sailor who took his guitar with him when he sailed with Columbus.

When I was a sailor in Palos, I played on my Spanish guitar, ping, ping! I used to sing songs to the ladies. —— I think of them still from afar, ping, ping!

Chorus: Ring, ping, ping! Ring, ping, ping! Ring out the bells, Oh, ring out the bells, Oh, ring out the bells! Ring, ping, ping! Ring, ping, ping! Ring out the bells, As I play on my Spanish guitar, ping, ping!

2. When my ship sailed out on the ocean, The sea was a hazard to sail, ping, ping! I couldn't sing toasts to the ladies, I had to hang over the rail, ping, ping! Chorus:

3. When my trip to the New World had ended, I returned home to Spain from afar, ping, ping! And I found the ladies all married; I'm all alone with my guitar, ping, ping! Chorus:

New text by R. Q.

HALLOWEEN

October 31

Long ago, the night before All Saints' Day was called "Hallow E'en"—meaning the eve of the hallowed, or holy, day. According to some ancient Celtic superstitions, on this night witches could fly, goblins and ghosts could roam, and certain humans could communicate with spirits.

Today, Halloween is very much a holiday for children. The most exciting time comes at dusk when the children dress in costumes and masks to go from door to door, calling out "Trick or treat!"

———

Program note: Ms. Bat will perform her entire act upside-down. The audience is requested not to snicker.

ACT XXI
Ms.
Bat

There Was a Li'l Woman Who Took a Stroll

This version of an old Kentucky ghost song is based on the English nursery tale, "The Teeny Tiny Woman."

1. There was a li'l woman who took a stroll, Ou-ou-ou-ou!
2. She stroll'd down by the old churchyard, Ou-ou-ou-ou!
3. She stroll'd right in the old graveyard, Ou-ou-ou-ou!
4. She saw a bone upon the ground, Ou-ou-ou-ou!

5. She took that bone a-layin' aground, Ou-ou-ou-ou!
6. She strolled'd back to her li'l abode, Ou-ou-ou-ou!
7. She went to the cupboard to hide the bone, Ou-ou-ou-ou!
8. She slowly turned the cupboard's key, Ou-ou-ou-ou!
9. She unlocked the door and———AAGH!

New text and music by R. Q.———————————————————

Watch out! Here come the witches! A song for group singing.

2. 1st group:
   Where are you witches a-going,
   A-going, a-going?
   Where are you witches a-going?
   Whippily, whoppily, WHOOP!

3. 2nd group:
   We're going trick-or-treating,
   Or-treating, or-treating,
   We're going trick-or-treating,
   Whippily, whoppily, WHOOP!

4. 1st group:
   And why would you want to do that,
   To do that, to do that?
   And why would you want to do that?
   Whippily, whoppily, WHOOP!

5. 2nd group:
   Because it's Halloween night,
   Hall'ween night, Hall'ween night,
   Because it's Halloween night,
   Whippily, whoppily, WHOOP!

NOTE: *You can make up other verses to this song, such as "Here come three monsters a-crawling," etc.*

New text by R. Q.

Skeleton Bones

This old American folk song has as its roots a famous spiritual.

quickly

Chorus:
Oh, those bones, oh, those bones, oh, those ske-le-ton bones, Oh, those bones, oh, those bones, oh, those ske-le-ton bones, Oh, those bones, oh, those bones, oh, those ske-le-ton bones, Oh, — good-ness, they scare!

Verse:
With the toe bone con-nect-ed to the foot bone, and the foot bone con-nect-ed to the ankle bone, and the ankle bone con-nect-ed to the leg bone, Oh, — good-ness, they scare!

2. With the leg bone connected to the knee bone,
   And the neck bone connected to the head bone,
   And the thigh bone connected to the hip bone,
   Oh, goodness, they scare!

3. With the hip bone connected to the back bone,
   And the back bone connected to the neck bone,
   And the neck bone connected to the head bone,
   Oh, goodness, they scare!

4. With the finger bone connected to the hand bone,
   And the hand bone connected to the elbow bone,
   And the elbow bone connected to the shoulder bone,
   Oh, goodness, they scare!

5. With the shoulder bone connected to the back bone,
   And the back bone connected to the neck bone,
   And the neck bone connected to the head bone,
   Oh, goodness, they scare!

Edited text by R. Q.

Little Ghost

This song, to the early 1800s tune of "Billy Boy," tells what happens when children go out in costume on Halloween night to knock on neighbors' doors.

New text by R. Q.

Jack-o'-lanterns

A Halloween song based on an old nursery tune.

very quickly

One lan-tern, Two lan-terns, Three jack-o'-lan – terns, Four lan-terns, Five lan-terns,

Six jack-o'-lan – terns, Sev-en lan-terns, Eight lan-terns,

Nine jack-o'-lan – terns, Ten lan-terns in a row!

2. Ten lanterns, Nine lanterns, Eight jack-o'-lanterns,
   Seven lanterns, Six lanterns, Five jack-o'-lanterns,
   Four lanterns, Three lanterns, Two jack-o'-lanterns,
   One standing all alone!

New text by R. Q.

Ten Little Goblins

Another Halloween song to the same tune. You can make up other variations for yourself.

1. One goblin, Two goblins, Three little goblins,
   Four goblins, Five goblins, Six little goblins,
   Seven goblins, Eight goblins, Nine little goblins,
   Ten goblins in a row!

2. Ten goblins, Nine goblins, Eight little goblins,
   Seven goblins, Six goblins, Five little goblins,
   Four goblins, Three goblins, Two little goblins,
   One goblin all alone!

96

New text by R. Q.

ELECTION DAY

The first Tuesday after the first Monday in November

Election Day is one of our most important holidays—the day when citizens exercise their right to decide who will govern them. Everyone can share in the excitement of listening to candidates and learning what they hope to do if elected.

Voting in secret began in the courts of Athens in ancient Greece. After a trial, each judge dropped a round stone into a box. A white stone meant "innocent," a black stone meant "guilty." In ancient Rome, voting was done by marking wax tablets with a pointed stick. Today voting in the United States is done at polling stations on a voting machine in a private booth.

———

Program note: In this act, Mr. Crow will show how to vote by secret ballot. Questions from the audience are encouraged.

ACT XXII

Mr. Crow

Ma! Ma! Where is Papa?

This amusing song is based on an 1884 song attributed to H. R. Monroe.

Edited text by R. Q.

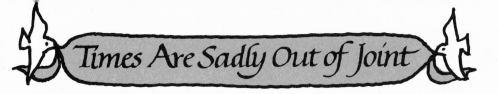

Times Are Sadly Out of Joint

This popular campaign song from the 1870s can be adapted in many versions for singing today.

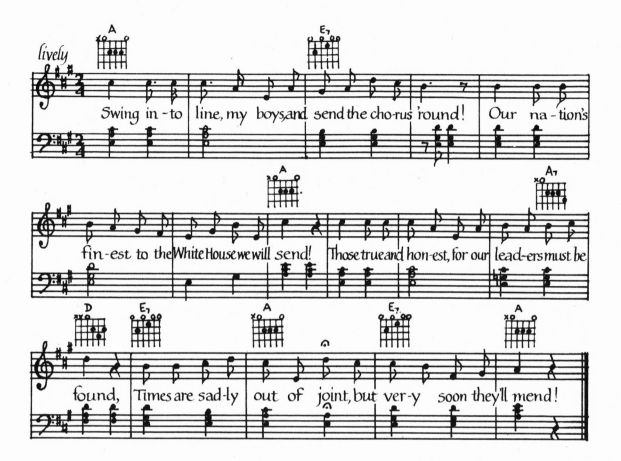

2. Swing into line, my girls, and join us at the poll!
Our nation's finest to the White House we will send!
Those true and honest we are seeking for this goal,
Times are sadly out of joint, but very soon they'll mend!

3. Come vote, vote, one and all, it is your right to do!
Our nation's finest to the White House we will send!
Vote for those leaders who are true and honest, too,
Times are sadly out of joint, but very soon they'll mend!

OTHER ADAPTATIONS
"Our nation's finest to the Congress we will send!,"
"Our nation's finest to the Senate we will send!,"
"Our finest judges to the Court House we will send!," etc.

Edited text and additional verses by R. Q.

For He's a Jolly Good Fellow

A traditional song that is sung during campaigning and election time. For women and girls, sing "For She's a Jolly Good Person"!

2. For she's a jolly good person, For she's a jolly good person,
   For she's a jolly good person, That nobody will deny.
   That nobody will deny, That nobody will deny.
   For she's a jolly good person, For she's a jolly good person,
   For she's a jolly good person, That nobody will deny.

Additional verse by R. Q.

VETERANS DAY

November 11

Veterans Day was originally called Armistice Day to commemorate the signing of the armistice agreement on November 11, 1918, that ended World War I. The holiday was observed with the hope that all wars had ended and that peace would last forever. Sadly, it lasted only twenty years. Many more United States soldiers lost their lives in a second World War, followed by the Korean War and the war in Vietnam. Therefore, Armistice Day was changed to Veterans Day to honor all who have served their country in the armed forces. The day is observed with parades, memorial services, and military concerts.

Program note: In this act, former Private First Class Thrush will demonstrate the art of peeling potatoes. French fry fanciers take note!

ACT XXIII
P.F.C. Thrush

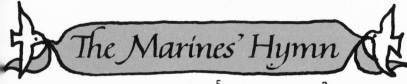

The Marines' Hymn

These words for the official song of the U.S. Marine Corps were probably written during the 1840s Mexican War by a Marine officer.

with spirit

From the Halls of Mon - te - - zu — ma To the shores of Tri-po – li, — We fight our coun-try's bat — tles On the land, in air, on sea. — First to fight for right and free — dom And to keep our hon-or clean; — We are proud to claim the ti – tle Of U-nit-ed States Ma - rine. —

102

Traditional text

The Caissons Go Rolling Along

The official song of the army's artillery corps.

2. To the front, day and night, Where the doughboys dig and fight, And the caissons go rolling along. Our barrage will be there, Fired on the rocket's flare, While those caissons go rolling along. Chorus:

Traditional text

103

You're in the Army Now

This traditional Army song is often sung by new soldiers as they march to their training fields.

lively

You're in the Ar - my now, — You're not— be-hind the plow; — You'll never get rich, By dig-ging a ditch, You're in the Ar - my now. — You're in the Ar - my now, — You're in the Ar - my now. — You'll never get rich, You'll never get rich, You're in the Ar - my now. —

Traditional text

Reveille

Sung to the notes of the morning bugle call, this is one of the many songs soldiers have invented to lift their spirits. The music is on page 72.

We got to get up, We got to get up, We got to get up this morning.
We can't get 'em up, We can't get 'em up, We can't get 'em up at all.
The corp'ral's worse than sergeants, The sergeant's worse than captains,
The captain's worse than colonels; And the bugler's worst of all!

Text adapted by R. Q.

THANKSGIVING DAY

The fourth Thursday in November

In 1621, when the Pilgrims had finally carved a home in America's wilderness with the help of friendly Indians, they looked at their harvest and felt it was time to rejoice and give thanks. The Wampanoag Indians, who had befriended the settlers, were invited to share the first Thanksgiving feast. It lasted for three days, and much wild turkey and venison was consumed. After that, the custom of holding Thanksgiving became a yearly event, though it was held at different times of the year in different parts of the country. It was not until President Lincoln's time that a date was set for national celebration of this holiday; it has been set each year ever since by presidential proclamation.

Program note: In this act, Mr. Turkey will strut for us. Be kind and give him a big hand.

Over the River and Thro' the Woods

For nearly one hundred years, this American folk song has been popular at Thanksgiving.

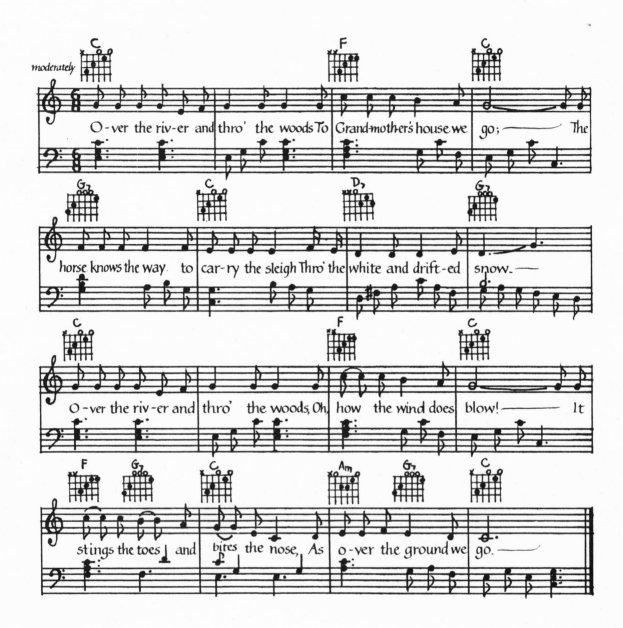

2. Over the river and thro' the woods,
   Trot fast, my dapple gray!
   Spring over the ground like a hunting hound,
   For this is Thanksgiving Day.
   Over the river and thro' the woods,
   Now Grandfather's face I spy!
   Hurrah for the fun! Is the turkey done?
   Hurrah for the pumpkin pie!

Traditional text

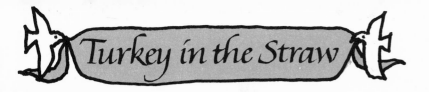

Turkey in the Straw

This song about our famous native bird is as American as Thanksgiving Day. It is perfect for square dancing and probably has a thousand verses in all its variations.

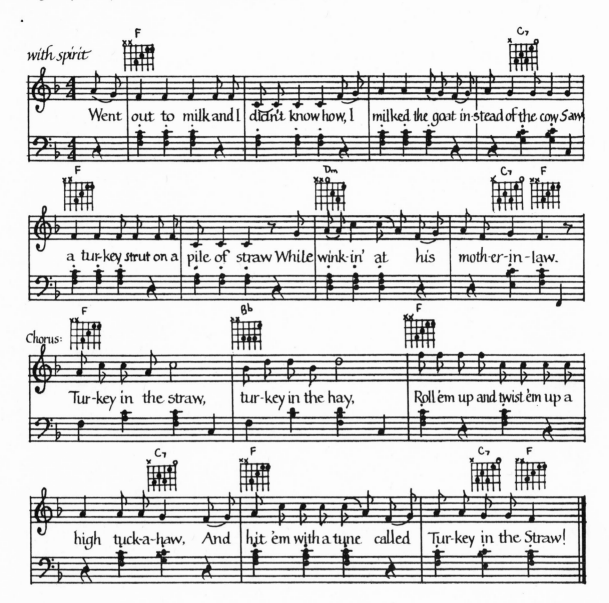

with spirit

Went out to milk and I didn't know how, I milked the goat in-stead of the cow Saw a tur-key strut on a pile of straw While wink-in' at his moth-er-in-law.

Chorus:

Tur-key in the straw, tur-key in the hay, Roll 'em up and twist 'em up a high tuck-a-haw, And hit 'em with a tune called Tur-key in the Straw!

2. Well, that old bird had a wooden leg,
   The best old turkey ever laid an egg.
   He laid more eggs than the hens on the farm,
   Thought layin' those eggs would do no harm.
                    Chorus:

New text by R. Q.

On the First Thanksgiving Day

A traditional American song for Thanksgiving Day singing.

2. On the first Thanksgiving Day,
Pilgrims bowed their heads to pray.
Thanked the Lord for food to share,
Thanked Him for a day so fair.
Now Thanksgiving comes again:
Praise the Lord as they did then;
Thank Him for our food to share,
Thank Him for a day so fair.

Additional verse by R. Q.

HANUKKAH

*Begins on the 25th day of the Hebrew month
of Kislev (usually in December)*

Hanukkah, the Jewish Feast of Dedication or Festival of
Lights, lasts for eight days. It commemorates the restora-
tion of the Temple of Jerusalem in the year 165 B.C., after
Judah Maccabeus had led a successful rebellion against
the Syrian rulers. When the Jews went to light the temple
lamps, they found only enough oil for one day—but mirac-
ulously, the light burned for eight days. Today at Hanukkah, families light candles in a branched candleholder
called a menorah—one the first night and one more on
each following evening. And for eight days there are special
foods to eat, blessings to be said, traditional songs to sing,
and gifts to be opened. It is one of the most joyful holidays
in the Jewish calendar.

---

*Program note: In this act, the Owl children will spin a dreydl. If it
should spin off the stage and into the audience, kindly return the
dreydl to the children.*

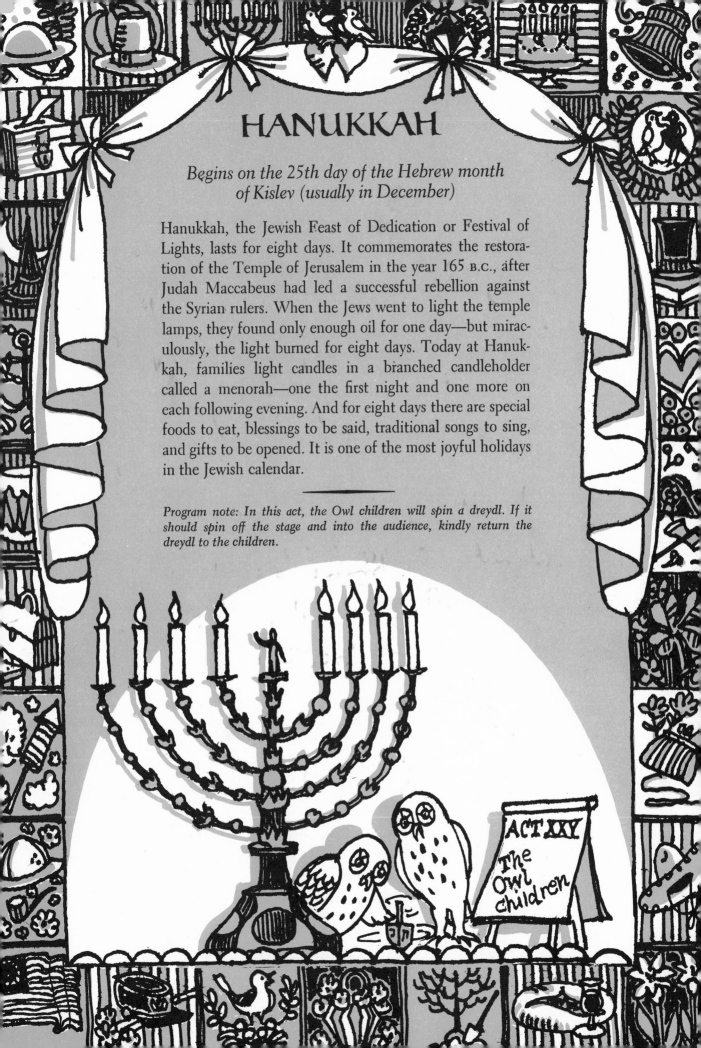

Hanukkah Song

The words to this popular Hanukkah song are sung to an old Yiddish folk melody.

horah: a circle dance
levivot: dumplings
s'vivonim: tops

See ACKNOWLEDGMENTS

My Dreydl

A dreydl is a special four-sided top with a Hebrew letter written on each side. It is traditional at Hanukkah for families to play various games with the spinning dreydl.

very lively

I have a lit-tle drey-dl, I made it out of clay, And when it's dry and read-y, Then drey-dl I shall play. Oh, drey-dl, drey-dl, drey-dl, I made it out of clay, Oh, drey-dl, drey-dl, drey-dl, Now read-y I shall play.

2. It has a lovely body,
With leg so short and thin,
And when it is all tired,
It drops and then I win.
Oh, dreydl, dreydl, dreydl,
With leg so short and thin,
Oh, dreydl, dreydl, dreydl,
It drops and then I win.

3. My dreydl, always playful,
It loves to dance and spin.
A happy game of dreydl,
Come play, now let's begin.
Oh, dreydl, dreydl, dreydl,
It loves to dance and spin,
Oh, dreydl, dreydl, dreydl,
Come play, now let's begin.

See ACKNOWLEDGMENTS

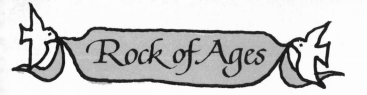

A traditional Hanukkah song that is sung to an ancient synagogal tune.

2. Kindling new the holy lamps, Priests, approved in suff'ring,
Purified the nation's shrine, Gave to God their off'ring;
And His courts surrounding Hear in joy abounding
Happy throngs singing songs With a mighty sounding.

112

Traditional text

CHRISTMAS

December 25

Christmas, around the world, is one of the happiest times of the year. It is a Christian holiday that celebrates Christ's birth, and it is also a family holiday when gifts are exchanged with warm feelings of love. Many beloved Christmas carols express the joy of this special day.

As people from many countries came to the United States, they brought with them their own Christmas traditions—foods, decorations, and especially songs. On the following pages are Christmas songs, some of which may be new to you; some come from different languages and traditions, but the spirit of love and happiness in all of them is the same.

Program note: In this act, Mr. Snow Bunting will show us how to wrap presents. That's something everyone needs to know!

ACT XXVI
Mr. Snow Bunting

The Star of Bethlehem

At Christmas in some parts of Italy, bagpipers serenade with this old Sicilian carol.

moderately

The night a Child was born — in Beth-le-hem-a-

far, — All through the night, there shone as bright as —

day — a star. Nev-er so bright-ly, nev-er so

light-ly shone a star — as on that night! This

gleam-ing star — sent — A bea-con to the

Wise — Men — in the O-ri-ent.

114

Edited text by R. Q.

Fum, Fum, Fum!

The word "fum" in this traditional Spanish carol is pronounced "foom," to imitate the sound of a strummed guitar.

SPANISH:

¡Viente-cinco de diciembre, fum, fum, fum!
¡Viente-cinco de diciembre, fum, fum, fum!
Nacido ha por nuestro amor,
El Niño Dios, Niño Dios,
Hoy de la Virgen Maria
En esta noche tan fria, ¡Fum, fum, fum!

Traditional text

115

Go Tell It On the Mountain

This famous spiritual has an irresistible hand-clapping rhythm.

2. While shepherds kept their watch
   O'er silent flocks that night,
   Behold! Up in the heavens
   They saw a holy light.
                    Chorus:

Traditional text

The Holy Child

A traditional Puerto Rican carol.

sadly

"Moth-er, see! A Child in our door-yard! He is beau - ti-ful! You
cold. And look! He is cry - ing For He has so lit - tle

see there? He is to wear." Then the moth - er brought Him in - side, Out from
asked Him where He came from And what

cold ev - er so gruel-ing. She
coun - try He was rul - ing. "My Fath-er is in

Heav-en, My Moth - er lives there, too; I'm

born to earth to suf-fer, To bring God's love to you!"

English version by R. Q.

117

O Christmas Tree

The Christmas tree, the most beloved feature of the Christmas celebration, began appearing in homes in Germany in the 15th century. This German folk song from the 1600s was written down in 1824 by Ernst Anshütz.

moderately

O Christ-mas Tree, O Christ-mas Tree, En-dur-ing are thy branch-es: So faith-ful green through-out the year, In sum-mer and when win-ter's here! O Christ-mas Tree, O Christ-mas Tree, En-dur-ing are thy branch-es!

2. O Christmas Tree, O Christmas Tree,
   Thy beauty is entrancing:
   At Christmastime, aglow with light,
   Thy presence fills us with delight!
   O Christmas Tree, O Christmas Tree,
   Thy beauty is entrancing!

3. O Christmas Tree, O Christmas Tree,
   Thy gentle spirit teaches us:
   That peace and love shall ever be
   As faithful as a Christmas tree!
   O Christmas Tree, O Christmas Tree,
   Thy gentle spirit teaches us!

GERMAN:
O Tannenbaum, O Tannenbaum,
Wie treu sind deine Blätter!
Du gürnst nicht nur zur Sommerszeit,
Nein, auch im Winter wenn es schneit.
O Tannenbaum, O Tannenbaum,
Wie treu sind deine Blätter!

118

2. O Tannenbaum, O Tannenbaum,
   Du kannst mir sehr gefallen!
   Wie oft hat nicht zur Weihnachtszeit
   Ein Baum von dir mich hoch erfreut!
   O Tannenbaum, O Tannenbaum,
   Du kannst mir sehr gefallen!

3. O Tannenbaum, O Tannenbaum,
   Dein Kleid soll mich was lehren!
   Die Hoffnung und Beständigkeit
   Gibt Trost und Kraft zu aller Zeit.
   O Tannenbaum, O Tannenbaum,
   Dein Kleid soll mich was lehren!

English version by R. Q.

There Was a Donkey Standing By

These words, sung to the melody of an old English Christmas carol, celebrate the gentle animals that gathered at the stable on the first Christmas.

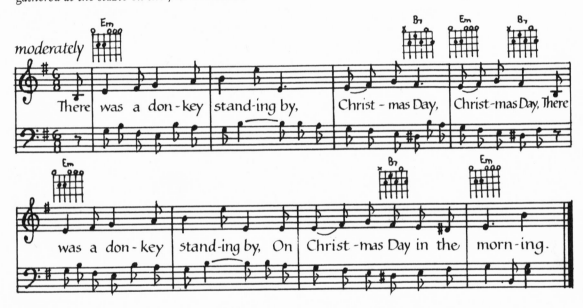

2. There was a camel standing by, Christmas Day, Christmas Day,
   There was a camel standing by, On Christmas Day in the morning.

3. There was a cow a-standing by, Christmas Day, Christmas Day,
   There was a cow a-standing by, On Christmas Day in the morning.

4. There was a dove coo-cooing by, Christmas Day, Christmas Day,
   There was a dove coo-cooing by, On Christmas Day in the morning.

5. There was a ewe baa-baaing by, Christmas Day, Christmas Day,
   There was a ewe baa-baaing by, On Christmas Day in the morning.

6. They came to see the Holy Child, Christmas Day, Christmas Day,
   They came to see the Holy Child, On Christmas Day in the morning.

Text by R. Q.

The Twelve Days of Christmas

The Twelve Days of Christmas lie between Christmas Day and Epiphany, January 6, when the three Wise Men offered the first Christmas presents—gold, frankincense, and myrrh. This old English carol celebrates the tradition of Christmas gift giving and receiving.

repeat as necessary

5. This fifth day of Christmas, My true love sent to me,
   Five gold rings, (Four calling birds, etc.)

6. This sixth day of Christmas, My true love sent to me,
   Six geese a-laying, (Five gold rings, etc.)

7. This seventh day of Christmas, My true love sent to me,
   Seven swans a-swimming, (Six geese a-laying, etc.)

8. This eighth day of Christmas, My true love sent to me,
   Eight maids a-milking, (Seven swans a-swimming, etc.)

9. This ninth day of Christmas, My true love sent to me,
   Nine pipers piping, (Eight maids a-milking, etc.)

10. This tenth day of Christmas, My true love sent to me,
    Ten drummers drumming, (Nine pipers piping, etc.)

11. This eleventh day of Christmas, My true love sent to me,
    Eleven lords a-leaping, (Ten drummers drumming, etc.)

12. This twelfth day of Christmas, My true love sent to me,
    Twelve ladies dancing, (Eleven lords a-leaping, etc.)

Traditional text

Christmas Day in the Morning

This is an old English nonsense song that is sung to the same tune as "There Was a Donkey Standing By" and many other songs, including "I Saw Three Ships."

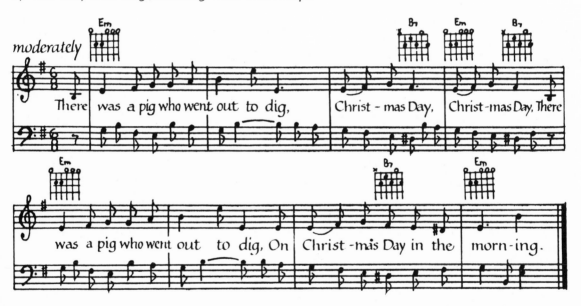

There was a pig who went out to dig, Christ - mas Day, Christ - mas Day, There was a pig who went out to dig, On Christ - mas Day in the morn - ing.

2. There was a crow who went out to mow, Christmas Day, Christmas Day,
   There was a crow who went out to mow, On Christmas Day in the morning.

3. There was a cow who went out to plow, Christmas Day, Christmas Day,
   There was a cow who went out to plow, On Christmas Day in the morning.

4. There was a doe who went out to hoe, Christmas Day, Christmas Day,
   There was a doe who went out to hoe, On Christmas Day in the morning.

5. There was a sheep who went out to reap, Christmas Day, Christmas Day,
   There was a sheep who went out to reap, On Christmas Day in the morning.

NOTE: *You can make up rhymes to tell what other animals do "On Christmas Day in the Morning."*

Edited text by R. Q.

Jolly Ol' Saint Nicholas

What is Christmas without a song about Santa Claus, otherwise known as Saint Nicholas? This cheerful song comes from the United States.

2. When the clock is striking twelve, When I'm fast asleep,
   Down the chimney broad and black With your pack you'll creep;
   All the stockings you will find Hanging in a row;
   Mine will be the shortest one, You'll be sure to know.

3. Johnny wants a pair of skates, Susy wants a drum;
   Judy wants a music book With tunes that she can hum;
   Don't forget my mother And father, both so dear;
   But choose for me, please, Santa Claus, Something nice this year.

Edited text by R. Q.

BIRTHDAYS

Birthdays come on any day of any month, and for the birthday boy or girl it's the best holiday of the year! It's a day for parties and presents, and for thinking about how it feels to be one year older. On your birthday it's traditional to make a wish and blow out the candles on the cake—
Happy Birthday!

———

Program note: In this act, Mr. Duck will demonstrate how to blow out birthday candles. Ushers must keep fire extinguishers handy.

Birthday Song

Here is a very special song just for birthday singing.

lively

Oh, Birth-day Pal* we sing-a-ling-a-ling With all our hearts to you, We

hope there'll be some-thing-a-ling-a-ling That we can do for you; In

au-tumn, win-ter, spring-a-ling-a-ling, And all the whole year through, This

lit-tle song we'll sing-a-ling-a-ling, A birth-day song for you!

* or the name of the person
whose birthday it is.

124

See ACKNOWLEDGMENTS

Additional text and music by H. B.

OTHER HOLIDAY SONGS TO SING

There was not enough space in this book to include all the other favorite holiday songs. But many that are not included may be easily found in other sources. On the next page you'll find a list of some other songs to sing at your holiday songfests.

———

Program note: By popular demand, Ms. Canary will sing all your other holiday requests. This ends our show—thank you for coming!

Other Songs To Sing

NEW YEAR'S DAY
A Happy New Year (to the tune of "Greensleeves")
We Wish You a Happy New Year (to the tune of "We Wish You a Merry Christmas")

DR. MARTIN LUTHER KING, JR'S. BIRTHDAY
The Old Rugged Cross
If I Can Help Somebody
Just a Closer Walk with Thee
Get Aboard, Little Children

ABRAHAM LINCOLN'S BIRTHDAY
Old Dan Tucker (one of Lincoln's favorite songs)
We Are Coming, Father Abra'am
Abraham's Daughter

VALENTINE'S DAY
My Funny Valentine (Rodgers & Hart)
You Are My Sunshine
A Bicycle Built for Two (Daisy Bell)

GEORGE WASHINGTON'S BIRTHDAY
Hail, Columbia! (Washington's Inaugural March)
God Save Washington

SAINT PATRICK'S DAY
Londonderry Air
MacNamara's Band
The Minstrel Boy
I Know Where I'm Goin'
The Gypsy Rover

APRIL FOOL'S DAY
I Know an Old Lady Who Swallowed a Fly
Pop! Goes the Weasel
The Animal Fair

PAN-AMERICAN DAY
Juanita
Alouette (French Canadian)
Oh, Canada!

EASTER
Easter Parade (Irving Berlin)
Here Comes Peter Cottontail
Easter Eggs! (Russian carol for Russian Easter)

PASSOVER
Adir Hu (Praise the Lord)
Chad Gadyo
Echod Mi Yodea (Who Will Sing Me?)

ARBOR DAY/EARTH DAY
Woodsman, Spare That Tree
The Ash Grove
In the Shade of the Old Apple Tree
Trees (Joyce Kilmer)

MAY DAY
Gathering Nuts in May

MOTHER'S DAY
I Want a Girl (Just Like the Girl That Married Dear Old Dad)
M-O-T-H-E-R

MEMORIAL DAY
The Battle Hymn of the Republic (page 18)
I Ain't Gonna Study War No More
Goober Peas
When This Cruel War Is Over

FLAG DAY
Rally 'Round the Flag, Boys
There Are Many Flags from Many Lands

FATHER'S DAY
The Happy Wanderer (My Father Was a Wanderer)
Oh, Mein Papa
Papa, Won't You Dance with Me?

INDEPENDENCE DAY
The Star-Spangled Banner (page 64)
Chester (page 25)
Ode to Independence Day
Hail, Columbia!

LABOR DAY
Home on the Range
Pick a Bale o' Cotton
Nine Pound Hammer
John Henry

AMERICAN INDIAN DAY
(See note on page 86)

COLUMBUS DAY
The Pinta, the Nina, and the Santa Marie (Hoagie Carmichael)
Sailing, Sailing

HALLOWEEN
The Devil and the Farmer's Wife
That Old Black Magic

ELECTION DAY
Happy Days Are Here Again
Hail to the Chief
Hello, Dolly (substitute your favorite candidate's name)

VETERANS DAY
The U.S. Air Force (Off We Go Into the Wild Blue Yonder)
Anchors Aweigh
Oh! How I Hate to Get Up in the Morning
K-K-K-Katy
There's a Long, Long Trail A-winding
Over There
Pack Up Your Troubles in Your Old Kit Bag
Keep the Home Fires Burning
When Johnny Comes Marching Home Again (page 61)
Tramp! Tramp! Tramp! (page 62)
Taps (page 62)
God Bless America

THANKSGIVING DAY
We Gather Together (Thanksgiving Hymn)
Lord, We Thank Thee
Doxology

HANUKKAH
Mi Y' Malel (Who Can Retell)
Hayo, Haya
B'rohos Shel Hanukkah

CHRISTMAS
Traditional Carols:
Silent Night
O Little Town of Bethlehem
Away in a Manger
It Came Upon a Midnight Clear
The First Noel
Hark! the Herald Angels Sing
Joy to the World
We Three Kings of Orient Are
O Holy Night
Adeste Fideles (O Come, All Ye Faithful)
Other popular songs:
We Wish You a Merry Christmas
Jingle Bells
Deck the Halls with Boughs of Holly
Up on the Rooftops (Ho Ho Ho)
Here Comes Santa Claus!
Rudolph, the Red-Nosed Reindeer
I'm Dreaming of a White Christmas

BIRTHDAYS
Happy Birthday to You!
For He's a Jolly Good Fellow (or "For She's a Jolly Good Person," page 100)

ABRAHAM LINCOLN'S BIRTHDAY, 15
America, 76
America the Beautiful, 74
AMERICAN INDIAN DAY, 83
APRIL FOOLS' DAY, 31
ARBOR DAY/EARTH DAY, 47
Arbor Day Song, 49
As I was a-walking one morning, 81
Auld Lang Syne, 10

Battle Hymn of the Republic, The, 18
Bells on New Year's Day, The, 9
Billy Boy, 22
Birthday Song, 124
BIRTHDAYS, 123
Blow the Man Down, 79

Caissons Go Rolling Along, The, 103
Chacarera, 37
Chester, 25
Christ the Lord is risen today, 40
CHRISTMAS, 113
Christmas Day in the Morning, 121
Cielito Lindo, 36
Cockles and Mussels, 29
COLUMBUS DAY, 87
Come all ye young fellows, 79
Come, Jeremy, Etan!, 44
Corn-Grinding Song (Zuñi), 85

Daddy Wouldn't Buy Me a Bow Wow, 68
Daddy's Whiskers (1), 70
Daddy's Whiskers (2), 71
Day is done, 62
Dayenu, 46
Deep in the Woods, 48
DR. MARTIN LUTHER KING, JR.'S BIRTHDAY, 11
Down the River, 82

EASTER, 39
Easter Basket, 42
Easter Hymn, 40
ELECTION DAY, 97
Erie Canal, 78

FATHER'S DAY, 67
FLAG DAY, 63
For He's a Jolly Good Fellow, 100
From la Sierra Morena, 36
From the Halls of Montezuma, 102
Fum, Fum, Fum!, 115

GEORGE WASHINGTON'S BIRTHDAY, 23
Git Along, Little Dogies, 81
Go Down, Moses, 45
Go Tell It on the Mountain, 116
Grandma, Grandma, have you heard?, 57

HALLOWEEN, 91
HANUKKAH, 109
Hanukkah Song, 110
He Knew the Earth Was Round-O, 88
Her name is Mary, 56
Here come three witches a-riding, 93
Here we come a-wassailing, 8
He's Got This Whole World in His Hands, 13
Holy Child, The, 117
Hurrah for the choice of the nation, 16
Hush, Little Baby, 57

I have a little dreydl, 111
I know you've heard of Washington, 26
I love my little cat, I do, 68
I'll give to you a paper of pins, 21
I'll sing to you about a man, 88
I'm a Yankee Doodle Dandy, 75
In Dublin's fair city, 29
INDEPENDENCE DAY, 73
Itisket, Itasket, 42
It's All Wrong, 89
It's the Same the Whole World Over, 50
I've Been Working on the Railroad, 80
I've got a mule, her name is Sal, 78

Jack-o'-lanterns, 96
Jolly Ol' Saint Nicholas, 122

LABOR DAY, 77
La Cucaracha, 38
Let tyrants shake their iron rod, 25
Lincoln and Liberty, 16 ·
Little Ghost, 95
Love My Daddy, Yes I Do, 71
Love Somebody, Yes I Do, 22

Ma! Ma! Where Is Papa?, 98
Mama's Gonna Buy, 57
Marines' Hymn, The, 102
Mary, 56
MAY DAY, 51
MEMORIAL DAY, 59
Michael Finnegan, 30
Michael, Row the Boat Ashore, 14

Mine eyes have seen the glory, 18
Mister Frog Went A-Courting, 20
"Mother, see! A Child in our dooryard," 117
MOTHER'S DAY, 55
My country, 'tis of thee, 76
My Dreydl, 111
My Mom Won't Allow, 58
My Spanish Guitar, 90

Navajo Happy Song, 84
NEW YEAR'S DAY, 7
No, No, Yes, Yes, Aria, The, 72
Now Is the Month of Maying, 53
O beautiful for spacious skies, 74
O Christmas Tree, 118
O Columbia, the gem of the ocean, 65
O Glorious Bells of Easter Day, 41
O Hanukkah, O Hanukkah, 110
Oh, Birthday Pal, 124
Oh, say, can you see, 64
Oh, those bones, 94
Oh, where have you been, little ghost?, 95
Ol' Abe Lincoln came out from the wilderness, 17
On December twenty-five, 115
On the first day of Christmas, 120
On the First Thanksgiving Day, 108
One goblin, two goblins, 96
One lantern, two lanterns, 96
OTHER HOLIDAY SONGS TO SING, 125
Out from the Wilderness, 17
Over hill, over dale, 103
Over the River and Thro' the Woods, 106

PAN-AMERICAN DAY, 35
Paper of Pins, A, 21
PASSOVER, 43
Peeping through the knothole, 33
Preparing for Seder, 44

Rain Dance (Zuñi), 86
Rain now is here with us, 86
Red, White, and Blue, The, 65
Reveille, 104
Rock of Ages, 112

Saint Patrick Was a Gentleman, 28
SAINT PATRICK'S DAY, 27
Say, where have you been, Billy Boy?, 22
Should auld acquaintance be forgot, 10
Sioux Night Song, 84

Skeleton Bones, 94
Star of Bethlehem, The, 114
Star-Spangled Banner, The, 64
Swing into line, my boys, 99

Taps, 62
Ten Little Goblins, 96
Tenting on the Old Camp Ground, 60
THANKSGIVING DAY, 105
The bells all toll, 9
The night a Child was born, 114
The river is deep, 82
There Was a Donkey Standing By, 119
There Was a Li'l Woman Who Took a Stroll, 92
There was a pig who went out to dig, 121
There was a young man named Michael Finnegan, 30
There's a Flea in Lizzie's Ear, 33
There's a Hole in Our Bucket, 32
This Ol' Man, 34
Three Little Girls, 52
Times Are Sadly Out of Joint, 99
Today's the First of May, 54
Tramp! Tramp! Tramp!, 62
Turkey in the Straw, 107
Twelve Days of Christmas, The, 120

VALENTINE'S DAY, 19
VETERANS DAY, 101

Washington the Great, 26
Wassail Song, 8
Watching for Pa, 69
We Can Overcome, 12
We got to get up, 104
We have a dear ol' daddy, 70, 71
Went out to milk and I didn't know how, 107
We're tenting tonight on the old camp ground, 60
When I was a sailor in Palos, 90
When Israel was in Egypt land, 45
When Johnny Comes Marching Home Again, 61
Whippily, Whoppily, Whoop, 93

Yankee Doodle, 24
Yankee Doodle Boy, 75
Yankee Doodle went to town, 24
Young and old are singing, 49
You're a Grand Old Flag, 66
You're in the Army Now, 104